Depositional Models of Shelf and Shoreline Sandstones

D1368621

Continuing Education Course Note Series #27

A Continuing Education Course Presented
at the 1983 AAPG Fall Education Conference

Thomas F. Moslow
Louisiana Geological Survey
Coastal Geology Program

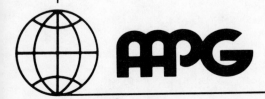

This book is an author-prepared publication
of the AAPG Education Program.

Extra copies of this, and other titles in the
Education Course Note Series, are available from:

The AAPG Bookstore
P.O. Box 979
Tulsa, Oklahoma 74101, USA

First Printing, December 1984

ISBN: 0-89181-176-1

TABLE OF CONTENTS

LIST OF SLIDES FROM OTHER SOURCES

THE SPEAKER ACKNOWLEDGES AND THANKS THE FOLLOWING:

Slide 8
Photograph by James Rine, ERCO, Inc.

Slide 24
Figure from D. G. McCubbin (1982).

Slide 26
Photograph by Larry G. Ward, Horn Point Environmental Laboratory.

Slide 28
Slide from C. Y. McCants, Getty Oil Company

Slide 30
Figure from D. G. McCubbin (1982).

Slide 32
Slide from R. W. Tillman, Cities Service Research

Slide 35
Figure from G. E. Reinson (1979).

Slide 43
Figure from R. S. Tye and T. F. Moslow (in press).

Slide 44
Photograph by M. O. Hayes, Research Planning Institute

Slide 46
Figure from A. G. Fischer (1961).

Slide 56
Figure from D. K. Davies, et al (1971).

Slide 57
Figure from A. A. McGregor and C. A. Biggs (1968).

Slide 58
Figure from K. P. Helmold, et al (1981)

Slide 59
Photograph by D. W. Jordan, Cities Service Research

Slide 60
Figure from D. K. Davies, et al (1971).

Slide 63
Figure from R. R. Berg and D. K. Davies (1968).

Slide 64
Figure from D. G. McCubbin (1982)

Slide 72
Photograph by M. O. Hayes, Research Planning Institute.

Slide 74
Figure from A. Wojtal-Duc and T. F. Moslow (1980).

Slides 79, 80, and 85
Figures and Photograph from R. J. Weimer and R. W. Tillman (1980).

Slide 81
Figure after J. K. Balsley (1980).

Slide 82
Figure after C. Land (1972).

Slide 86
Photograph by S. D. Heron, Jr., Duke University

Slides 98, 101, 102, and 106
Figures from R. S. Tye (1984) and T. F. Moslow and R. S. Tye (1984).

Slide 99
Photograph by M. O. Hayes, Research Planning Institute

Slides 100, 103, and 107
Photographs by R. S. Tye, Louisiana Geological Survey

Slides 108-117
Figures from R. J. Weimer and R. W. Tillman (1982)

Slide 125
Figure from D. J. P. Swift (1976).

Slide 133
Figure from D. G. McCubbin (1982).

Slides 134, 135, 136, 140, 141, 151, and 152
Figures from R. W. Tillman and R. Martinsen (1984).

Slides 137 and 138
Figures from J. M. Boyles and A. J. Scott (1981).

Slides 142-150
Figures and Photographs from R. S. Tye, et al (1983) and C. L. Hearn, et al (1984).

Slides 156 and 158
Photographs by S. Penland, Louisiana Geological Survey

Slides 159-162
From J. S. Suter, T. F. Moslow and S. Penland (1983).

Slide 164
Figure from K. A. Dickinson, et al (1972)

Slide 165
Figure from A. J. Scott

Slide 166
Figure from A. G. Fischer (1961).

Slide 167
Figure from R. J. Weimer and R. W. Tillman (1982).

Slides 168, 169, and 171-179
Figures from S. Penland and J. S. Suter (1983) and S. Penland,
    J. S. Suter, and R. Boyd (1982).

Slide 180
Figure from D. G. McCubbin and M. J. Brady (1969), in D. G. McCubbin
    (1982).

Slide 184
Figure from W. A. Wescott (1983).

ACKNOWLEDGEMENTS

The author gratefully acknowledges his association with present and former members of the Cities Service Sedimentology Research Group especially Rod Tillman, Jim Ebanks, Roger Slatt, Jim Rine, Doug Jordan, Bob Tye, Mike Boyles, Robin Lighty and Ken Helmold. The interchange of ideas and concepts with these individuals has been invaluable towards the development of depositional models presented in this lecture series.

Much of the information on barrier islands and tidal inlets is derived from research ventures with Miles O. Hayes, S. Duncan Heron, Jr. and Robert S. Tye.

Shea Penland and John Suter of the Louisiana Geological Survey, Coastal Geology Program, provided valuable information concerning the evolution and seismic-stratigraphic character of deltaic barrier island shoreline and inner-shelf depositional systems. Judy Golson and Cheryl Roussel typed the course notes.

Ted Beaumont of AAPG is thanked for his encouragement and advice in the preparation of this lecture series.

INTRODUCTION

Scope and Objectives

This lecture course is designed to provide geologic insights towards the development of depositional and exploration models for sandstone reservoirs associated with one or more of a variety of shelf and shoreline environmental settings. Sedimentologic and stratigraphic criteria will be utilized to more accurately predict the subsurface distribution and trend of reservoir quality sandstones. These criteria include a number of basic geologic "tools" such as well logs, cores, outcrop, seismic, and isopach and structure maps, all of which will be utilized in varying degrees during this course. Equally important in the development of models for shelf and shoreline sandstones is the subsurface analysis of modern depositional systems. An understanding of the three dimensional framework of modern clastic sedimentary environments is critical to the proper interpretation of vertical sequences, lateral facies relationships, sand body geometries and inhomogeneities of sandstone reservoirs.

Geologic Tools

Listed below are some of the fundamental geologic "tools" used in the development of models for shelf and shoreline sandstones as presented in this course:

1) <u>Analysis of modern clastic depositional systems</u> through examination of:
   - processes of sedimentation
   - geomorphology of sedimentary deposits
   - cores of subsurface sediments
   - high resolution seismic profiles.

These analyses allow for the development of a depositional model or modern analogue, as outlined in Figure
1, and can be extremely valuable in the exploration or
production of ancient clastic reservoirs.

MODERN CLASTIC SYSTEMS

ANALYSIS OF:

PROCESSES	**CORING**
GEOMORPHOLOGY	**SEISMIC**
HISTORY	**CHRONOLOGY**

YIELDS:

DEPOSITIONAL MODEL

Figure 1

2) Process Sedimentology. This is a methodology
   for analyzing clastic sediments in such a way
   that the observed sedimentary structures (i.e.
   cross-bedding and burrowing) are correlated to
   depositional processes. The goal with this type
   of sedimentological approach is to more accurately
   interpret the depositional environment in which
   the clastic sediments being examined were deposited.

3) Outcrop analysis of ancient sequences as the surface
   expression of a subsurface sandstone reservoir to
   provide the following criteria:
     - facies relationships
     - variations in vertical sequences
     - lateral geometries of sand bodies
     - permeability and porosity barriers
     - reservoir inhomogenities
     - reservoir trend and thickness

4) <u>Core and cuttings analysis</u>, including the comp-
   osition, texture, mineralogy, physical and biogenic sedimentary structures, and variations
   in permeability and porosity of cored sequences
   in subsurface sandstone reservoirs.

5) <u>Analysis of electric and radioactive well logs</u>
   for the purposes of predicting:
   - reservoir quality
   - distribution of reservoir fluids
   - oil-water contacts

Also, the correlation of cores to specific log responses is extremely useful in constructing subsurface
stratigraphic cross-sections and outlining better reservoir
quality facies.

In summary, the analyses of the above mentioned
"geologic tools" yield certain products, such as isopach
and structure maps, vertical sedimentary sequences and stratigraphic cross-sections (Fig. 2). When these products are
combined with a carefully developed depositional model of a
clastic reservoir, some most-valuable insights can be
gained to enhance exploration or production activities.

Figure 2

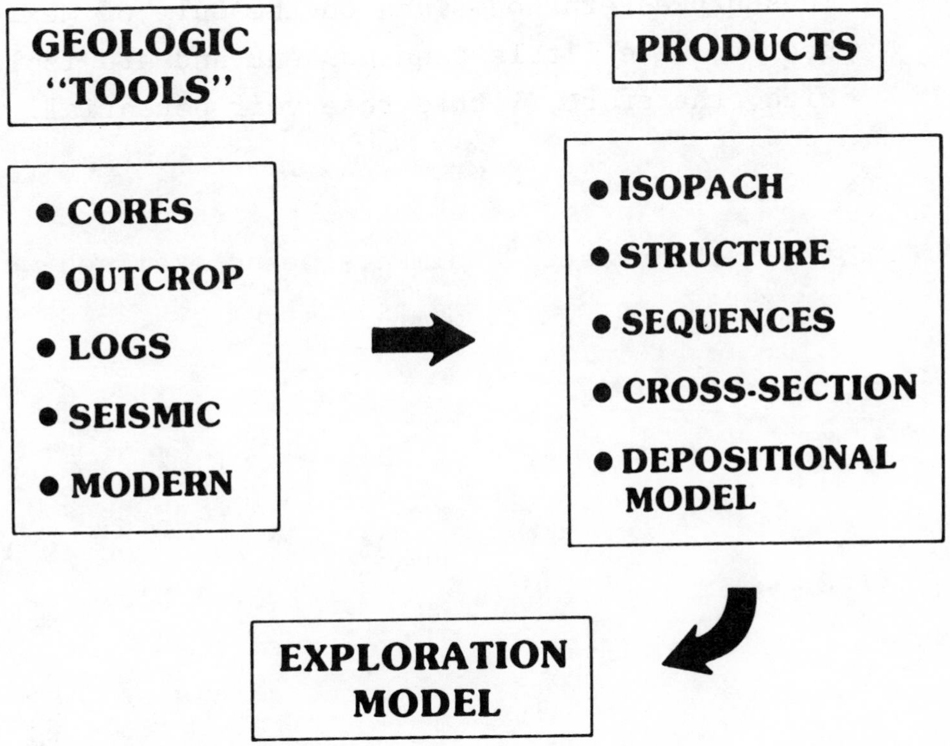

GEOLOGIC "TOOLS"

- CORES
- OUTCROP
- LOGS
- SEISMIC
- MODERN

PRODUCTS

- ISOPACH
- STRUCTURE
- SEQUENCES
- CROSS-SECTION
- DEPOSITIONAL MODEL

EXPLORATION MODEL

DEPOSITIONAL SYSTEMS (An Overview)

Within the realm of terrigenous clastic depositional systems there exists a broad spectrum of varying depositional environments. Because of physical limitations and the scope of this study, only shelf and shoreline depositional systems will be examined. Therefore, emphasis is placed in this short course on Barrier Island, Tidal Inlet, Shoreface and Inner Continental Shelf Sand bodies in both deltaic and non-deltaic settings.

Those clastic shoreline environments of deposition that are not examined in detail in this study, but may serve as modern analogues for some sandstone reservoirs include: beach-ridge strand plains, chenier plains, sandy tidal flats and estuaries. However, it should be noted that beach-ridge strand plains have many affinities to prograding barrier islands, which are examined in detail within the framework of this course. Also, tidal flats and estuaries are referred to in the discussion of barrier island lagoons and tidal inlets. Lastly, chenier plain environments like those investigated in southwestern Louisiana on the Gulf of Mexico shoreline seem to have little sand content and are isolated features with, therefore, little reservoir potential.

BARRIER ISLAND SHORELINE SYSTEMS

Introduction:

Over the past decade, subsurface studies on modern
shorelines, primarily on the U.S. Gulf and East coasts,
have provided the basis for significantly more sophist-
icated barrier island shoreline models. These studies
have documented the effects of wave energy, tidal range
and storms in determining sedimentary sequences and sand
body geometry. Facies relations and preservation potential of barrier islands are controlled by sea-level fluctuations and sediment supply. Shoreline orientation is
controlled by structural setting and antecedant topography.

As a result of Holocene sea level rise, most modern
barrier islands are transgressive, and are characterized
by thin sequences of burrowed lagoonal muds overlain by
horizontally bedded washover-foreshore sands of storm
origin. Transgressive barriers have a sheet-like geometry,
low preservation potential and are rarely recognized in
ancient deposits. Although less common in modern settings,
seaward prograding (regressive) barrier islands are highly
depositional and characterized by thick, coarsening-up
sequences of burrowed to crossbedded fine sand. Regressive
barriers have a lenticular geometry, thicken and fine
seaward, and are common reservoirs. The shore-parallel
migration of tidal inlets results in significant reworking
of both types of barrier island, deposition thick fining-
up sequences of cross-bedded coarse sand. Inlet deposits
can account for up to 50% of Holocene barrier shorelines
and have a greater preservation potential than most other
barrier-associated facies. Inlet geometries vary from

wedge (wave-dominated) to U-shaped (tide-dominated).

Best reservoir potential and thickest sand accumulations occur in the shoreface and tidal inlet associated facies. Upper shoreface to foreshore facies are dominantly an orthoquartzitic, well sorted, fine-medium sand with little or no detrital clays due to winnowing and lack of burrowing. Tidal inlet channels-and-deltas may be similar lithologically except they include poorly sorted fine-to-coarse sand and shell.

Modern shoreline studies have greatly enhanced recognition of ancient barrier sequences and predication of reservoir distribution and behavior. Cretaceous barrier island reservoirs in the Western Interior include the Muddy Sandstone and Almond Formation at Patrick Draw Field. Micro-to-mesotidal strike oriented regressive barriers and dip oriented cross-barrier sand bodies are observed.

This section will examine both the modern day depositional systems and some ancient counterparts from the Cretaceous Western Interior of North America to provide insights for the development of barrier island shoreline models.

Controls on Sedimentation and Stratigraphy

The stratigraphy and evolution of any barrier island depositional system is determined by its long-term response to several factors. The most important of these include: sea level fluctuations, variations in sediment supply, pre-depositional topography, tectonic setting (basin submergence or emergence), and hydrographic regime (Fig. 3). The relative importance of these controlling factors can vary greatly from one barrier to the next. Tidal range, wave energy, storms and inlet migration are the major shoreline

CONTROLS ON SHORELINE SEDIMENTATION

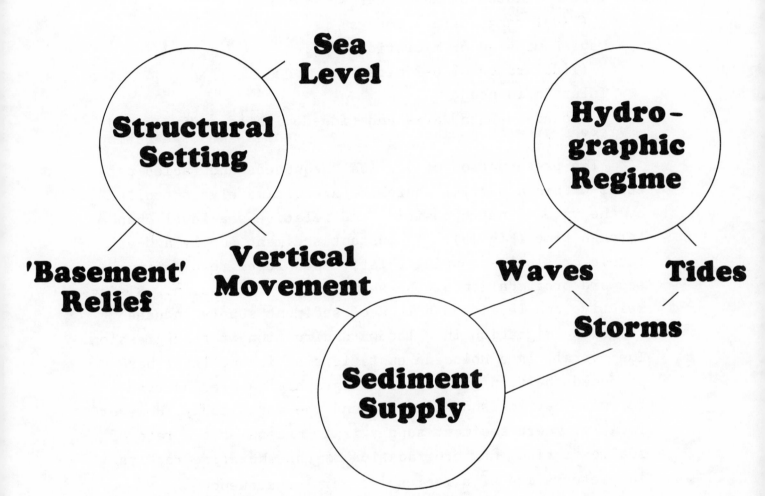

Fig. 3. Major depositional controls on sedimentation in clastic shoreline environments.

processes that determine the presence, morphology and lateral distribution of specific sedimentary sequences and sand body geometries within a barrier island system (Fig. 4). These processes yield what is referred to in this text as Process Models for barrier shorelines:

- Tide-Dominated or Mesotidal
  (Tidal range of 2-4 meters)
- Wave-Dominated or Microtidal
  (Tidal range of 0-2 meters)
- Inlet Influenced
  (found in both wave- and tide-dominated environments).

The preservation of vertical sequences and facies patterns within a barrier shoreline are ultimately controlled by the rate of net deposition and relative sea level change through time (Fig. 5). A constant sediment supply and a stable or slowly-dropping relative sea level results in seaward progradation of the shoreline or regression. Rising relative sea level and a lack of sediment supply induces shoreline migration in a landward direction or transgression. The overall late Holocene eustatic rise in sea level has produced the transgressive stratigraphic nature observed for most barrier shorelines around the world today. However, locally, where sediment supply is in excess of the rate of sea level rise, net progradation of the shoreline results in preservation of a regressive barrier sequence.

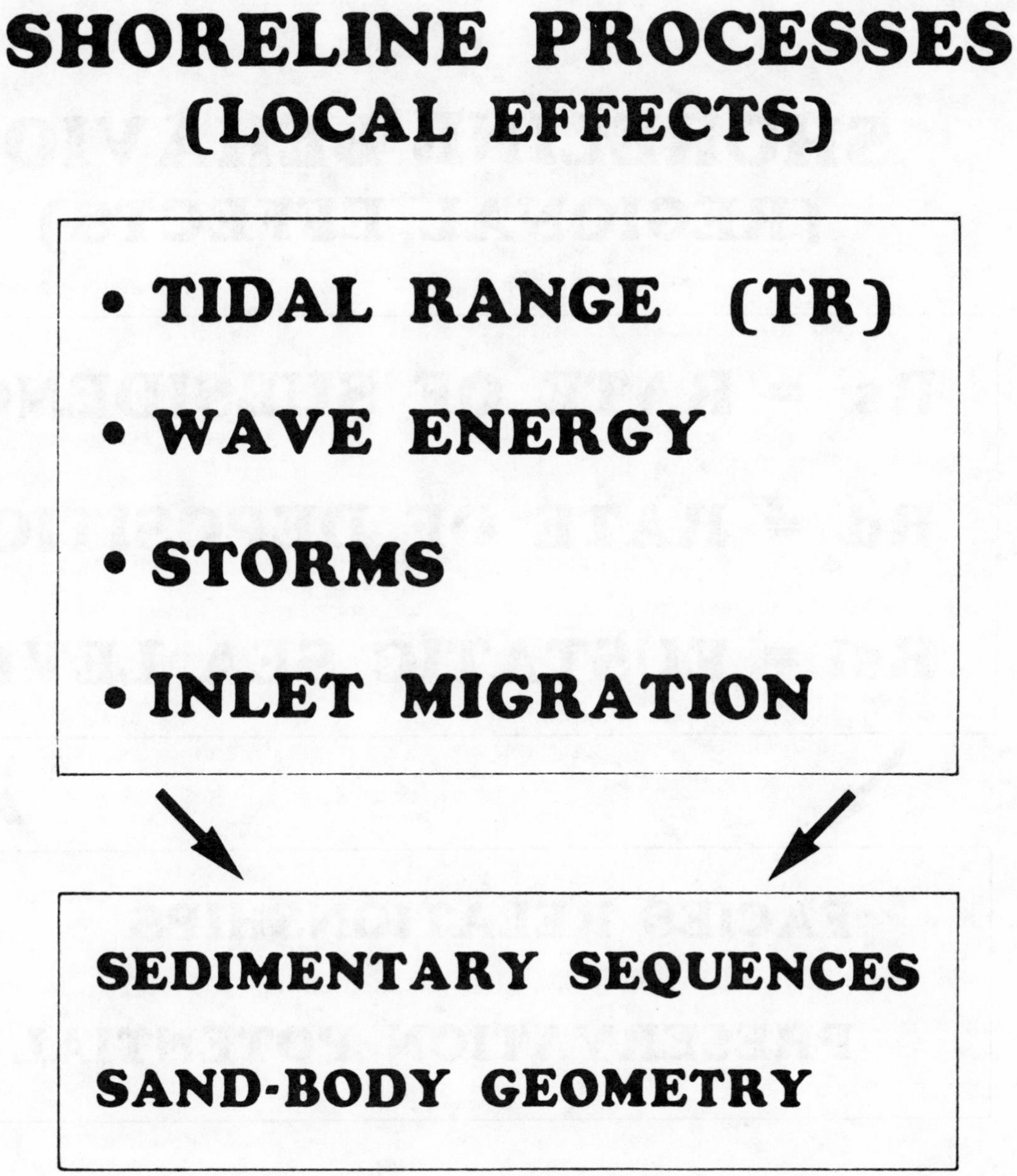

SHORELINE PROCESSES
(LOCAL EFFECTS)

- **TIDAL RANGE (TR)**

- **WAVE ENERGY**

- **STORMS**

- **INLET MIGRATION**

SEDIMENTARY SEQUENCES

SAND-BODY GEOMETRY

Fig. 4. Major depositional processes that produce the observed sedimentary sequences and sand-body geometries in barrier island systems.

SHORELINE BEHAVIOR
(REGIONAL EFFECTS)

R_s = RATE OF SUBSIDENCE

R_d = RATE OF DEPOSITION

R_{sl} = EUSTATIC SEA LEVEL

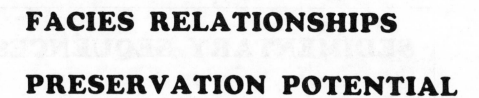

FACIES RELATIONSHIPS

PRESERVATION POTENTIAL

Fig. 5. Major regional controls effecting barrier shoreline behavior and resultant facies relationships and their preservation potential.

Stratigraphic Models depicting facies relationships of barrier island shorelines are shown in Fig. 6.
All three stratigraphic models are a function of sea
level change, rate of subsidence and rate of deposition.
These stratigraphic models are diagrammatically explained
in Fig. 6 and are used to categorize the barrier shoreline systems examined in this course.

Environments of Deposition

The different types of depositional environments
associated with a barrier island shoreline are shown in
Fig. 7.   The main trend of a barrier island is a strike-
oriented linear sand body referred to as the "barrier-
beach complex" (Fig. 7).   Barrier islands are often
broken by channels which convey water tidal exchange
from the lagoon or bays behind the barrier island and
the shoreface or inner shelf waters seaward of the
barrier.   These breaks or channels, along the island
are referred to specifically as tidal inlets.   These
inlets tend to migrate laterally along the shoreline
reworking the sediments previously deposited.

The inlets are associated with very large deltaic
sandbodies that are called ebb-tidal deltas on the seaward side of the inlet, and are deposited by ebb-tidal
currents and waves.   On the landward side of the barrier
inlets are associated with flood-tidal deltas, which are
formed by tidal currents.

The interaction of wave regime and tidal range has
a profound effect not only on morphology, but also on
the migration and stratigraphy of tidal inlets and barrier
islands.   A contrasting geomorphic character (occurrence,

STRATIGRAPHIC MODELS

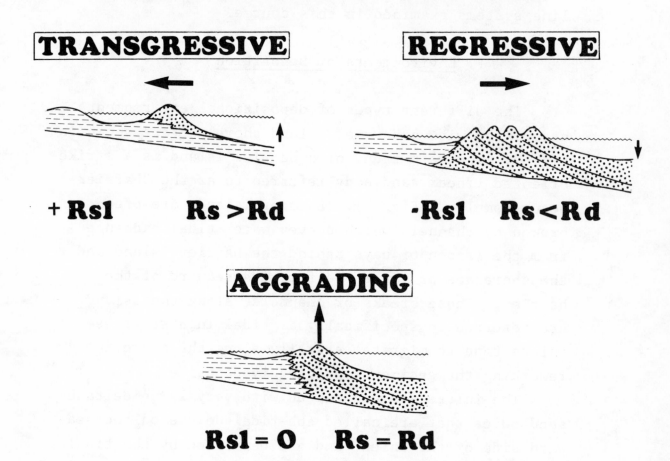

Fig. 6. Stratigraphic models for clastic barrier shorelines as a function of the rate of sea level change (Rsl),
rate of subsidence (Rs) and rate of deposition (Rd).

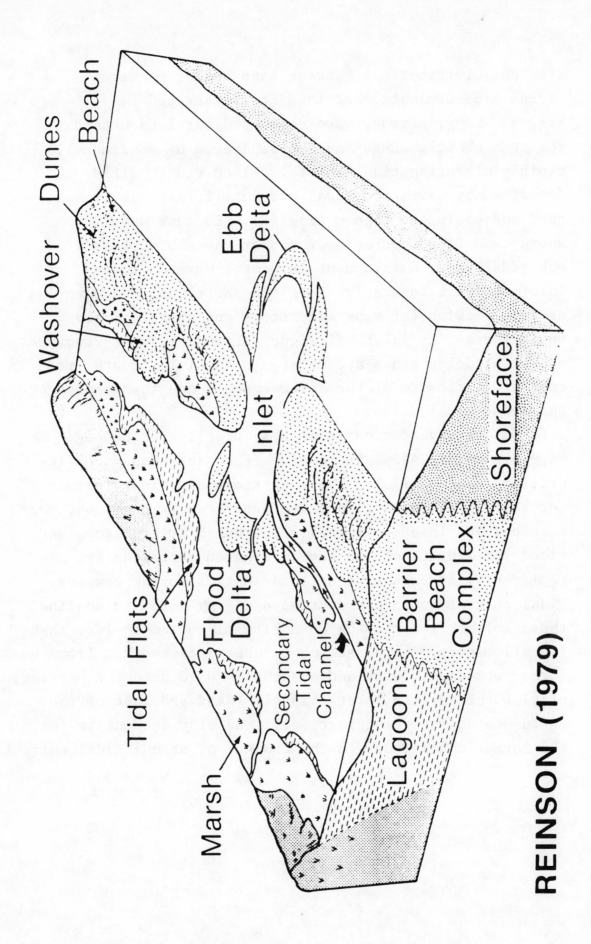

REINSON (1979)

Fig. 7. Block diagram displaying the depositional environments associated with a barrier island shoreline (after Reinson, 1979).

-13-

site and distribution) between sand bodies in wave-
versus tide-dominated settings is illustrated in
Fig. 8. Long, narrow, wave-dominated barriers extend
for tens of kilometers and are separated by ephermeral,
rapidly migrating tidal inlets. Flood-tidal deltas
deposited by waves and tidal currents form large, lobate
sand bodies in the lagoon (Fig. 8). Because wave
energy and flood currents overpower the ebb currents,
ebb-tidal delta development is poor. Wave-dominated
inlets migrate laterally along the shoreline in a downdrift direction for many kilometers and at relatively
rapid rates. As inlet efficiency decreases, wave-reworked
ebb-tidal delta sands accumulate in the inlet mouth, resulting in closure of the inlet channel and abandonment of
the flood-tidal delta.

Unlike wave-dominated coasts, tidally-influenced
barriers often assume a stunted, drumstick-shaped configuration (Hayes, 1975). These barriers are wider, extend
for several kilometers, and are separated by numerous, more
stable tidal inlets (Fig. 8). The backbarrier lagoon and
flood-tidal delta of the wave-dominated shoreline are
replaced by an expansive salt marsh-tidal creek complex.
Tidal current dominance over wave energy helps to confine
these inlets, restricting downdrift migration to less than
two kilometers. Large sediment lobes are reworked from the
former ebb-tidal delta and eventually weld onto the barrier,
closing the earlier inlet channel. Landward, out of the
influence of wave transport, silt and clay accumulate in
the former channel due to the absence of strong tidal currents.

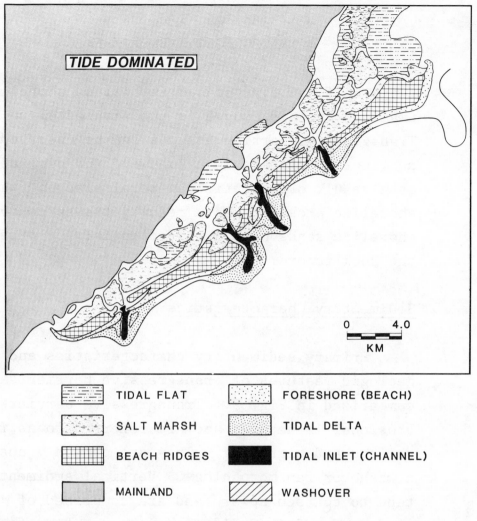

TIDE DOMINATED

0   4.0
KM

	TIDAL FLAT		FORESHORE (BEACH)
	SALT MARSH		TIDAL DELTA
	BEACH RIDGES		TIDAL INLET (CHANNEL)
	MAINLAND		WASHOVER

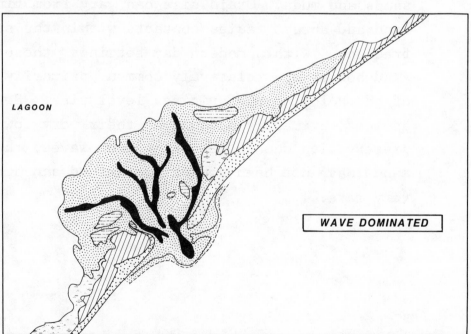

LAGOON

WAVE DOMINATED

Fig. 8. Distribution of depositional environments associated with barrier islands and tidal inlets in wave-dominated and tide-dominated shorelines (from Moslow and Tye, 1984).

TRANSGRESSIVE BARRIERS

The first type of barrier island shoreline to be examined in this course is the transgressive type. Transgressive barrier islands can be observed in modern settings to migrate in a landward (up dip) direction as a result of eustatic sea level rise and wave-induced shoreline erosion. As a result, transgressive barrier shoreline sands have a low potential for preservation in the rock record.

Sedimentary Characteristics

Primary sedimentary characteristics and major geologic features of transgressive barrier sands are summarized in Fig. 9. Transgressive barriers are generally erosional in nature, and are referred to as retrograding or landward migrating. They are commonly characterized by a washover fan morphology. Vertical sedimentary sequences tend to coarsen upward and are comprised of interbedded sands and muds. Grain size can vary from fine to coarse sand and abrupt facies contacts within the sand body are frequent. Within modern day settings, these types of sand bodies are relatively common, primarily as a result of the Holocene eustatic sea-level rise. However, in the ancient, primarily because of their very low potential for preservation due to reworking from waves, these barrier sands have not been commonly observed and are generally very rare.

TRANSGRESSIVE BARRIERS

EROSIONAL (RETROGRADING) WASHOVER MORPHOLOGY COARSENING-UP SEQUENCE

INTERBEDDED SAND + MUD
F-C GRAINED
ABRUPT CONTACTS

MODERN → "COMMON"
ANCIENT → "RARE"

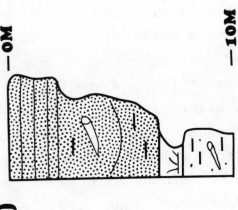

—0M

—10M

Fig. 9. Characteristic geologic features of modern transgressive barrier islands.

Modern Example

The barrier islands comprising the Cape Lookout cuspate foreland, North Carolina, are excellent examples of transgressive barrier sands in a wave-dominated (microtidal) environment (Fig. 10). The barriers are relatively long, linear and narrow and backed by wide shallow, open, lagoons. Tidal inlets are rare and ephemeral, but migrate laterally at very high rates (Moslow and Heron, 1978). Tidal inlets on the higher-energy northeast barrier limb (Core and Portsmouth Banks) are associated with large flood-tidal deltas and small ebb deltas (Fig. 11). The most prominent aspects of barrier morphology on Core and Portsmouth Banks are the extensive wash-over fans, fringing salt marsh and wide open lagoons. Storm overwash processes, in conjunction with shore-line erosion from a rising sea level, has resulted in the landward migration of Core and Portsmouth Banks over the past several thousand years (Fig. 12).

Depositional Units:

Unconformably overlying the Pleistocene lagoonal deposits along the entire length of Core Banks is a diverse sequence of Holocene barrier deposits. The average depth of occurrence for the Holocene/Pleistocene contact is generally about -9 m MSL. The sequence of Holocene sediments averages from 10-12 m in thickness. Holocene sediments beneath Core Banks have been divided into three depositional units: barrier, back-barrier, and migrating inlet. These typically fossilliferous, fine- to coarse-grained, tan to light gray sands and silts are represented by nine different depositional environments. A description of the character-istic sediments associated with each depositional environment is given in Table 1.

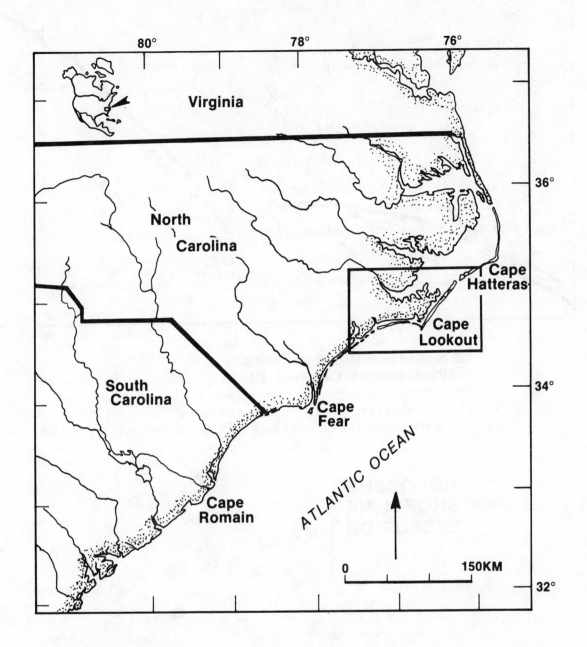

Fig. 10. Location map of the Cape Lookout cuspate foreland, North Carolina (from Heron et al, 1984).

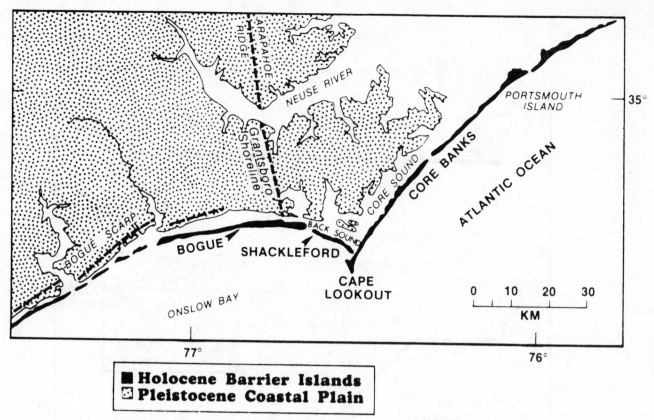

Fig. 11. Location of barrier islands forming the
Cape Lookout cuspate foreland (from Heron et al, 1984).

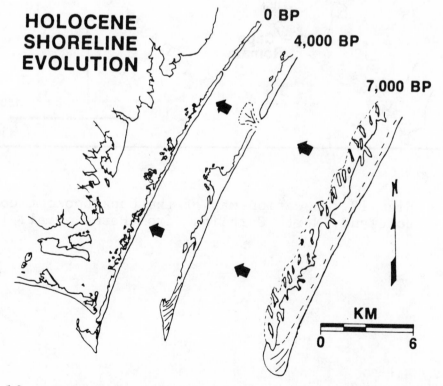

Fig. 12. Stages in the late Holocene evolution of Core
Banks. The diagram shows the relative distance offshore,
and paleogeomorphology of the barrier at 7,000 and 4,000
years BP based on computed rates of landward migration
(from Moslow and Heron, 1979).

Table 1. Transgressive Barrier Island Facies Characteristics

Depositional Environment	Lithology	Shells and Organics	Sedimentary Structures	Large Scale Features
Overwash and Foreshore	Clean, mod. sorted fine to med. sand	Whole and abraded shells in layers; variable assemblage (low diversity)	Horizontal and planar laminations	Caps inlet and barrier sequences
Shoreface	Well sorted, fine to med. sand and silt	Abundance of sand-sized shell material *Gemma gemma*, *Arcopecten* sp., *Olivella* sp	Cross-bedded (upper half) and burrowed (lower half) sequence	Coarsening upward sequence; increase in mud content towards base.
Backbarrier (lagoon, tidal flat, salt marsh)	Well sorted, fine to med, silty sand and sandy clay	Organic rich: *Spartina* sp. and other plant material; *Ensis* sp., *Crassostrea* sp., *Crepidula* sp. mollusks)	Burrowed; thin parallel clay laminations	Capped by salt marsh; increasing mud and organic content upwards
Flood-Tidal Delta	Mod. sorted, med. to coarse silty sand	Coarse shell frags, common; Echinoderm frags. common	Gently dipping cross-laminae; burrowed	Interbedded with backbarrier facies; cyclic fining upward sequences

Facies Relationships:

The Holocene sediments beneath Core Banks reveal
a complex depositional history dominated by barrier
retreat, spit extension and inlet migration. A transgressive sequence of sediments dominates the Holocene
stratigraphy. The common occurrence of barrier overwash sands overlying backbarrier silty-sands and salt
marsh peats indicate that landward migration has been
an active process in the island's evolution. However,
in five isolated sections, the Holocene section has
been completely reworked by the action of migrating
tidal inlets (Fig. 13).

The five relict inlets found beneath Core Banks
are typically represented by three depositional facies.
These are: (1) inlet floor, (2) main channel, and
(3) inlet margin (spit platform). The inlet floor and
main channel sediments form the migrating inlet proper
and represent the bulk volume of inlet-fill. Approximately
15% of the Holocene sediments beneath Core Banks are
inlet-related deposits (Moslow and Heron, 1978). The
inlet-fill deposits displace Holocene backbarrier
silty-sands and are overlain by medium- to coarse-grained
washover sands (Fig. 13). Tidal inlet depositional
models are discussed in detail in a later section of
these notes.

Recognition and Preservation:

Transgressive barriers do not form an easily
recognizable thick vertical sequence of sediments.
Transgressive barriers are underlain by about 10 m of
lagoon, marsh, tidal flat, flood delta and overwash-
foreshore sands with some silts and muds (Fig. 14).
Lagoon, marsh, tidal flat and flood delta facies are
not really characteristic of the barrier island per se

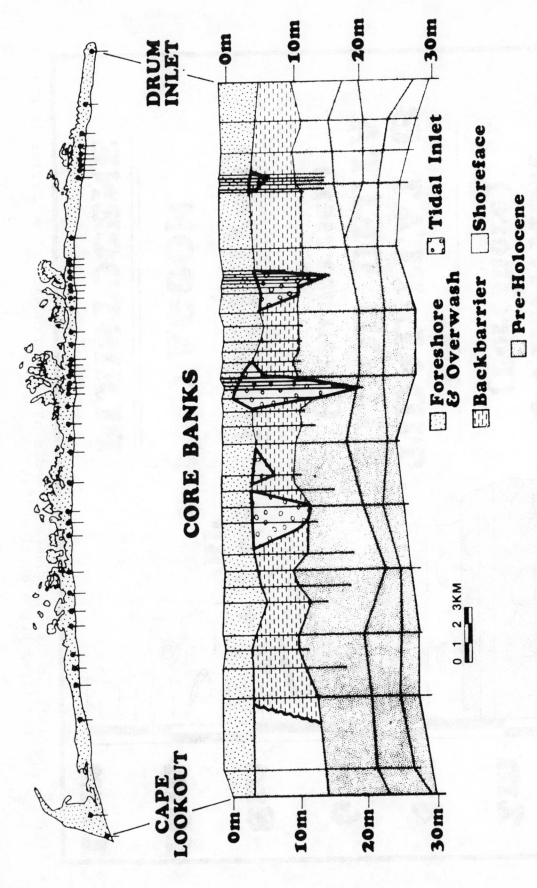

Fig. 13. Shore-parallel (strike oriented) cross-section of the transgressive Core Banks, North Carolina barrier island system. Note discrete tidal inlet channel deposits in subsurface (after Moslow and Heron, 1978).

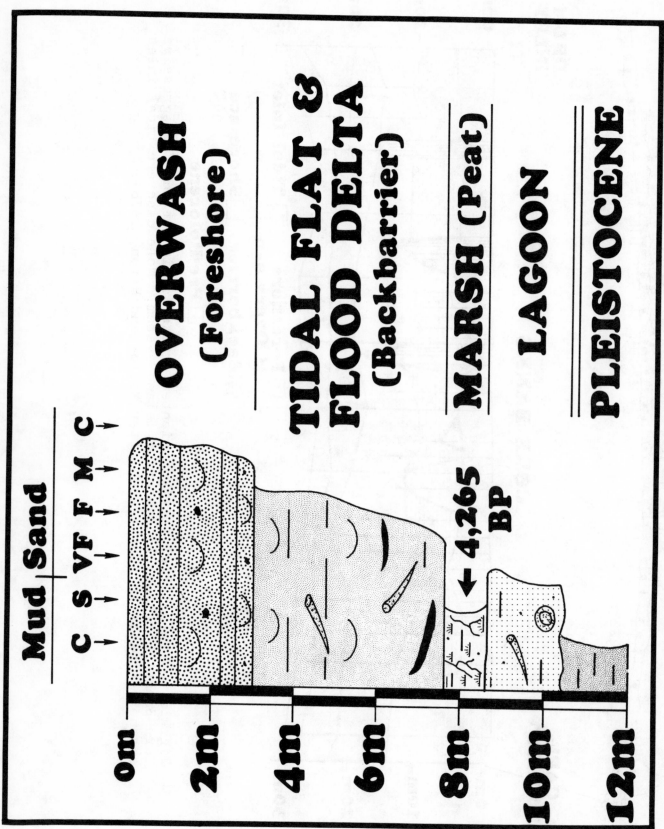

Fig. 14. Typical vertical sequence of sediments in a transgressive barrier island system (from Heron et al., 1984).

although they may be associated with a barrier shore-line. The transgressive barrier proper consists of 2-3 m of overwash-foreshore sands as linear bodies. Associated facies occur as non-linear or arcuate-shaped sand bodies (that is, flood-tidal deltas), overlying widespread lagoonal silts and muds. Thus, even though the trans-gressive barrier has a "typical" vertical sequence (Fig. 14) recognition of ancient barriers would be difficult based on observation of this sequence along. The presence of fining upward inlet sequences associated with the other barrier-related facies would be the clue to identifying ancient transgressive barriers.

Preservation of transgressive barrier island sequences depends on a high rate of sand accumulation and on subsidence capable of progressively burying the deposits. The occurrence of barriers and lagoons on modern, depositional and actively subsiding coastal areas, suggests that similar coastal en-vironments probably existed in the past.

Three features of transgressive barriers deposits make them attractive as exploration objectives:

1. They are typically composed of clean, well-sorted, parallel-laminated sand with good primary porosity;
2. They are associated with organic-rich, fine grained lagoonal sediments which may provide excellent source rocks;
3. They "pinch out" up-dip into fine-grained lagoonal sediments so they provide excellent stratigraphic traps.

Stratigraphic models of sand body geometry and char-acteric log response for transgressive barrier shorelines in wave and tide dominated settings are shown in Fig. 15. Transgressive barrier sands are relatively thin and lenti-cular in strike and dip sections. This type of geometry was classically referred to as "sheet-like" or "shoestring sands". The sands pinch out up-dip and thicken in a down dip (seaward) direction (Fig. 15). Along strike, trans-gressive barrier sand bodies display thick, frequent coarse-grained inlet-fill sequences.

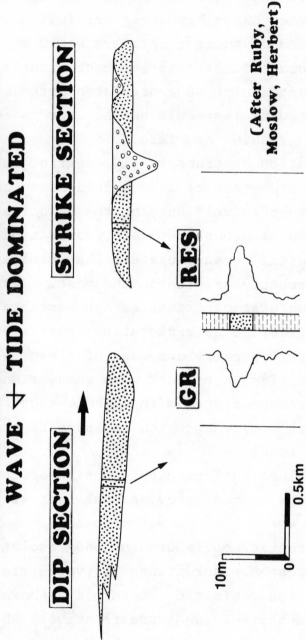

Fig. 15. Sand-body geometry and characteristic log response for transgressive barrier shorelines in wave and tide dominated settings.

Ancient Example

Although transgressive barrier island deposits
can be recognized in ancient sedimentary sequences, there
are few occurrences reported in the literature. Transgressive barrier sands have been recognized in outcrop
(i.e., the Pennsylvanian of Eastern Kenturky), as well as
in the subsurface (Cretaceous of Montana) (Berg and Davies
1968; McGregor and Biggs, 1968; Horne and Ferm, 1976).

Bell Creek Field lies in southeastern Montana,
Powder River County (Fig. 16). The Cretaceous Muddy
Formation in Bell Creek Field has been interpreted as
a barrier island sequence that is, at least in part,
transgressive in nature (Berg and Davies, 1968; Davies
et al, 1971). Well locations are shown on an isopach
map of the Muddy Formation (Fig. 17). This isopach is
similar in morphology to that of a modern transgressive
barrier island chain. The arcuate shaped sandstone
body that extends updip (paleo-landward) into lagoonal
shales is interpreted as a series of storm washover
deposits (Fig. 17). The extreme thickness and lateral
extent of the washover sandstone in the Muddy is related to the vertical stacking and lateral overlapping
of numerous individual washover deposits.

The Muddy Sandstone in Bell Creek Field consists
of a barrier island sequence with transgressive washover
fan deposits which produce oil up-dip and pinch out
into lagoonal fine-grained sediments. Two cores described
by Berg and Davies (1968) from Bell Creek Field are
depicted in Figs. 18 and 19. Gary 22-6 (Fig. 18) was
cored through the barrier island sequence, while Gary
6-14 (Fig. 19) was cored through the back-barrier washover
sequence. This well is just off the location map (Fig.
17) to the southwest.

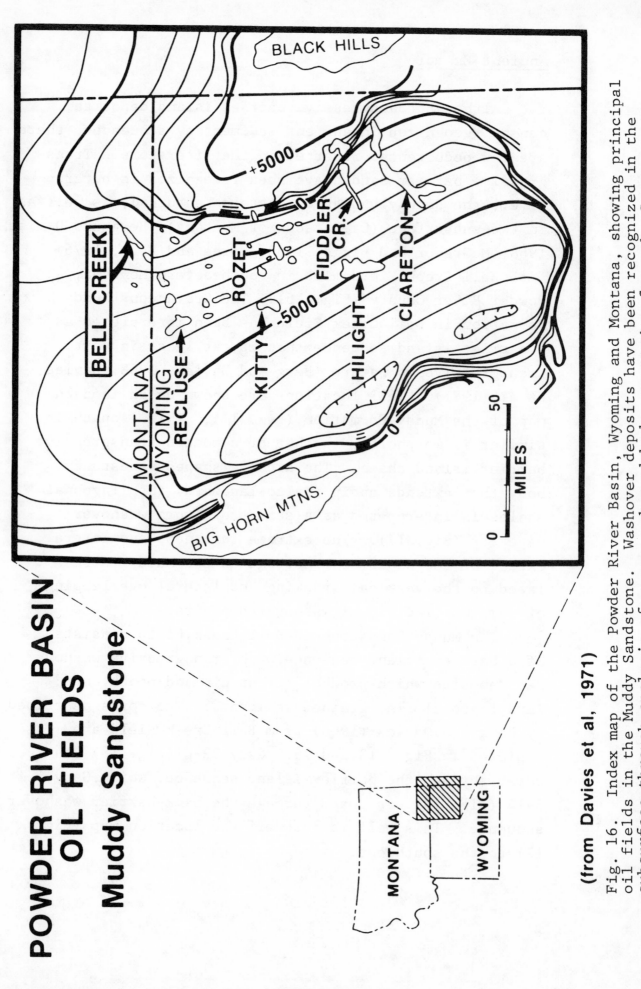

POWDER RIVER BASIN OIL FIELDS
Muddy Sandstone

(from Davies et al, 1971)

Fig. 16. Index map of the Powder River Basin, Wyoming and Montana, showing principal oil fields in the Muddy Sandstone. Washover deposits have been recognized in the subsurface through analysis of cores and sand body geometries from the Cretaceous Muddy Sandstone at Bell Creek Field, Montana (Davies et al, 1971).

MUDDY ISOPACH - BELL CREEK FIELD
R 54 E

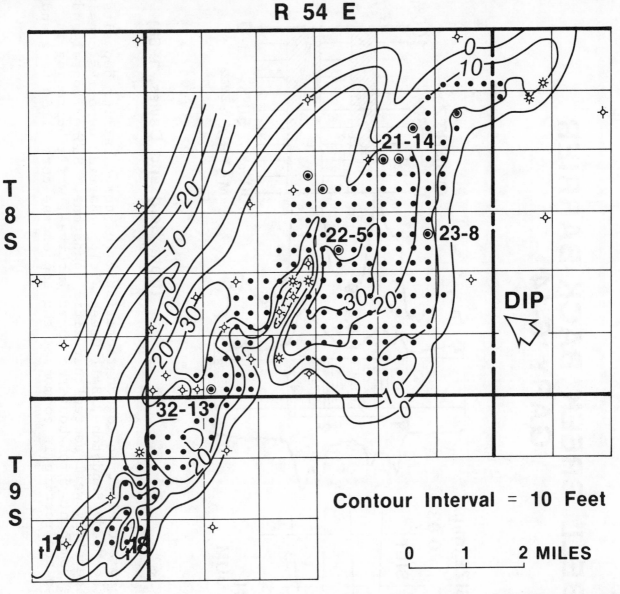

Contour Interval = 10 Feet

0   1   2 MILES

(after McGregor and Biggs, 1968)

Fig. 17. Isopach of the Muddy Sandstone at Bell Creek
Field showing linear barrier island sandstones partly
overlapped in the center of the field. Regional dip is
to northwest (arrow). Note the thin arcuate fan of
"washover" sandstone that extends updip (paleo-landward)
into lagoonal deposits. The washover sandstone is comprised of a
series of stacked washover deposits interbedded with lagoonal
siltstones and silty shales. Location of cores of washover sandstone utilized in this study are shown (from Berg
and Davies, 1968). Note location of the Gary 22-5, Taack
No. 11 (t11) and No. 18 (t18) wells. Gary 6-14 is off this
diagram to the southwest (from McGregor and Biggs, 1968).

BELL CREEK BACK-BARRIER GARY 6-14

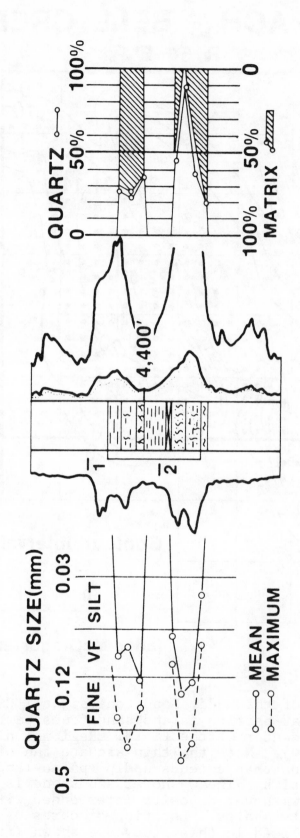

(from Berg and Davies, 1968)

Fig. 18. Sedimentary and electric log characteristics of cored barrier deposits from Gary 6-14 in the Muddy Sandstone, Bell Creek Field. Barrier deposits consist of fine-grained, moderately well sorted quartzitic sandstone. Subhorizontal and massive bedding are dominant throughout the cored interval, while burrowing is common near the base and rooting is common at the top of the core (from Berg and Davies, 1968).

-30-

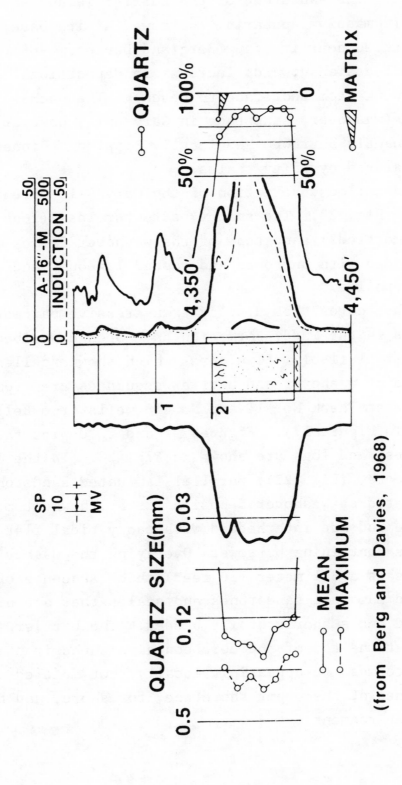

Fig. 19. Sedimentary and electric log characteristics of cored back-barrier (washover) deposits from Gary 22-5 in the Muddy Sandstone, Bell Creek Field. Washover deposits are fine-grained moderately well sorted quartzitic sandstone. Horizontal laminations are dominant and burrowing and rooting are common at the top and base of the washover unit (from Berg and Davies, 1968).

Note that in both wells, the mean quartz size (about 0.25 mm) and the quartz content (90%) are roughly equal, reflecting a similar origin of the deposits. The sandstone of the barrier island sequence is massive-appearing, burrowed at its base, and root-mottled near its top (Berg and Davies, 1968). This reflects an upwards increase in depositional energy (shallowing from shoreface to beach). The back-barrier (washover) sandstone in Gary 6-14, however, is predominantly burrowed and locally rippled, thinner, and separated by silty shales.

A detailed description of the Gary 6-14 core is shown in Fig. 20. The shaley, structureless (root and burrow mottled?) sandstone of the washover facies is interbedded with burrowed and rooted lagoonal and marsh deposits.

Other cores that display transgressive barrier deposits in the Muddy Formation have been described by Jordan et al (1981). Two cores which show excellent examples of washover and barrier sequences are from the Midwest Taack No. 11 and No. 18 wells from Bell Creek (shown in Figure 17). Figures 21 and 22 depict the two cores, and logs are shown in Fig. 23. In the Taack No. 18 core, (Fig. 21), parallel-laminated sandstone interpreted as washover deposits lie at the bottom of the core and are interbedded with sandy tidal flat deposits containing burrows. Overlying the washover deposits is a 3.1 meter (10 feet) thick sequence of tidal flat and lagoonal sandstones and shales that are bio-turbated and subhorizontally bedded. The barrier island facies at the top of the core contains subhorizontally bedded to massive-appearing, locally root-mottled sandstones of the upper shoreface, foreshore, and back-shore environments.

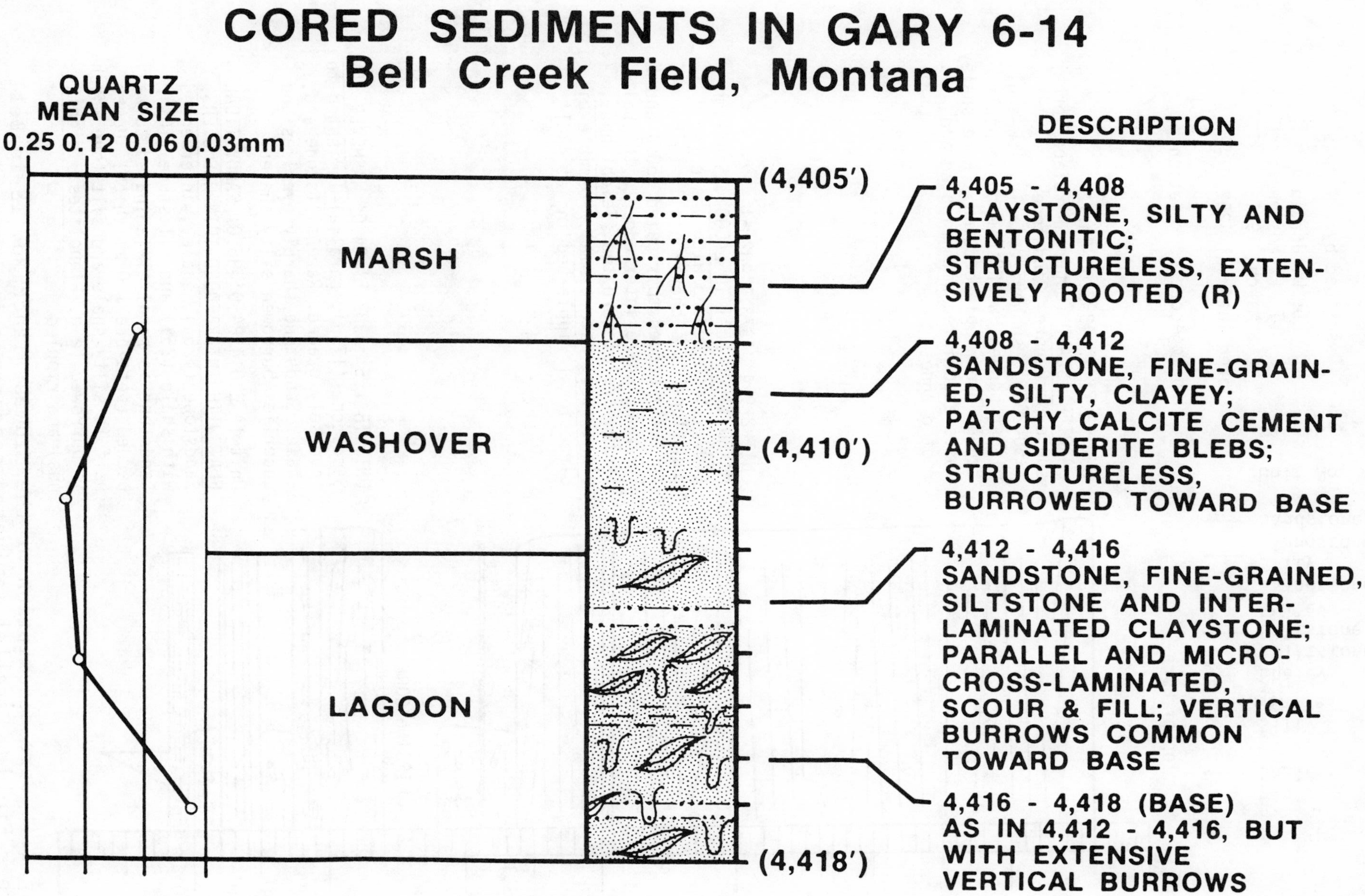

CORED SEDIMENTS IN GARY 6-14
Bell Creek Field, Montana

DESCRIPTION

4,405 - 4,408
CLAYSTONE, SILTY AND BENTONITIC; STRUCTURELESS, EXTENSIVELY ROOTED (R)

4,408 - 4,412
SANDSTONE, FINE-GRAINED, SILTY, CLAYEY; PATCHY CALCITE CEMENT AND SIDERITE BLEBS; STRUCTURELESS, BURROWED TOWARD BASE

4,412 - 4,416
SANDSTONE, FINE-GRAINED, SILTSTONE AND INTERLAMINATED CLAYSTONE; PARALLEL AND MICRO-CROSS-LAMINATED, SCOUR & FILL; VERTICAL BURROWS COMMON TOWARD BASE

4,416 - 4,418 (BASE)
AS IN 4,412 - 4,416, BUT WITH EXTENSIVE VERTICAL BURROWS

(4,405')

(4,410')

(4,418')

MARSH

WASHOVER

LAGOON

QUARTZ
MEAN SIZE
0.25 0.12 0.06 0.03mm

Fig. 20. Sedimentary structures, textures, and lithology of cored sediments in Gary 6-14, Bell Creek Field, Montana. A thin, massive to laminated washover sandstone occurs between rooted, marsh claystone above and burrowed, lagoonal siltstones and claystones below (from Davies et al., 1971).

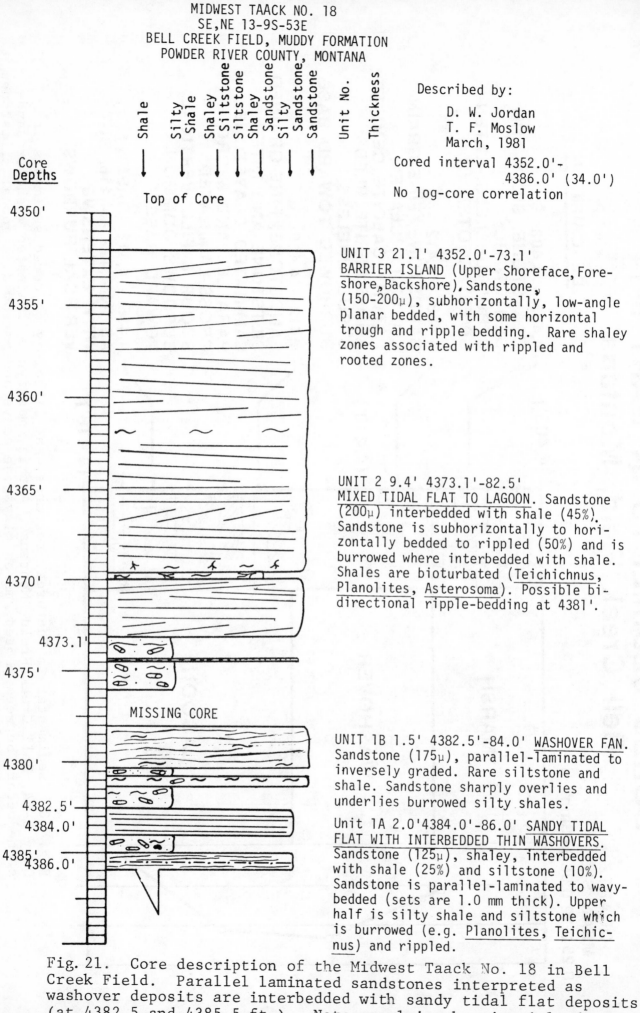

MIDWEST TAACK NO. 18
SE,NE 13-9S-53E
BELL CREEK FIELD, MUDDY FORMATION
POWDER RIVER COUNTY, MONTANA

Described by:

D. W. Jordan
T. F. Moslow
March, 1981
Cored interval 4352.0'-
4386.0' (34.0')
No log-core correlation

Shale
Silty Shale
Shaley Siltstone
Siltstone
Shaley Sandstone
Silty Sandstone
Sandstone
Unit No.
Thickness

Core Depths

Top of Core

4350'
4355'
4360'
4365'
4370'
4373.1'
4375'
MISSING CORE
4380'
4382.5'
4384.0'
4385'
4386.0'

UNIT 3 21.1' 4352.0'-73.1'
BARRIER ISLAND (Upper Shoreface,Fore-shore,Backshore), Sandstone,
(150-200μ), subhorizontally, low-angle planar bedded, with some horizontal trough and ripple bedding. Rare shaley zones associated with rippled and rooted zones.

UNIT 2 9.4' 4373.1'-82.5'
MIXED TIDAL FLAT TO LAGOON. Sandstone (200μ) interbedded with shale (45%). Sandstone is subhorizontally to hori-zontally bedded to rippled (50%) and is burrowed where interbedded with shale. Shales are bioturbated (Teichichnus, Planolites, Asterosoma). Possible bi-directional ripple-bedding at 4381'.

UNIT 1B 1.5' 4382.5'-84.0' WASHOVER FAN. Sandstone (175μ), parallel-laminated to inversely graded. Rare siltstone and shale. Sandstone sharply overlies and underlies burrowed silty shales.

Unit 1A 2.0'4384.0'-86.0' SANDY TIDAL FLAT WITH INTERBEDDED THIN WASHOVERS. Sandstone (125μ), shaley, interbedded with shale (25%) and siltstone (10%). Sandstone is parallel-laminated to wavy-bedded (sets are 1.0 mm thick). Upper half is silty shale and siltstone which is burrowed (e.g. Planolites, Teichic-nus) and rippled.

Fig. 21. Core description of the Midwest Taack No. 18 in Bell Creek Field. Parallel laminated sandstones interpreted as washover deposits are interbedded with sandy tidal flat deposits (at 4382.5 and 4385.5 ft.). Note overlying barrier island sequence resulting from transgression (from Jordan et al, 1981).

MIDWEST TAACK NO. 11
NW,SE 14-9S-53E
Bell Creek Field, Muddy Formation, Powder River County, Montana

Described by: D. W. Jordan
T. F. Moslow
(March, 1981)

Cored interval 4305-4326.7
(21.7')
Core to log correction=log is
4.0' deeper.

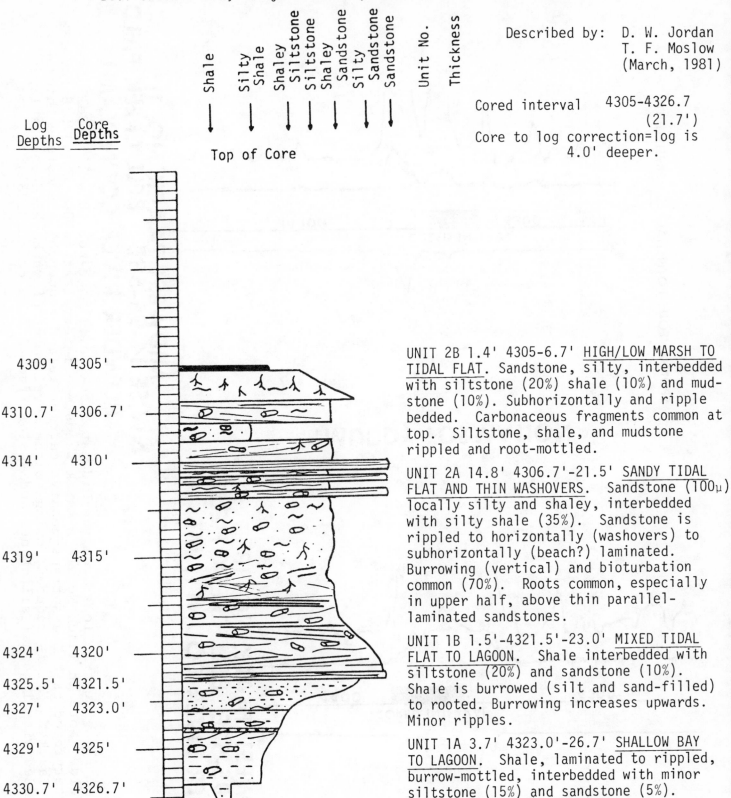

UNIT 2B 1.4' 4305-6.7' HIGH/LOW MARSH TO TIDAL FLAT. Sandstone, silty, interbedded with siltstone (20%) shale (10%) and mudstone (10%). Subhorizontally and ripple bedded. Carbonaceous fragments common at top. Siltstone, shale, and mudstone rippled and root-mottled.

UNIT 2A 14.8' 4306.7'-21.5' SANDY TIDAL FLAT AND THIN WASHOVERS. Sandstone (100µ) locally silty and shaley, interbedded with silty shale (35%). Sandstone is rippled to horizontally (washovers) to subhorizontally (beach?) laminated. Burrowing (vertical) and bioturbation common (70%). Roots common, especially in upper half, above thin parallel-laminated sandstones.

UNIT 1B 1.5'-4321.5'-23.0' MIXED TIDAL FLAT TO LAGOON. Shale interbedded with siltstone (20%) and sandstone (10%). Shale is burrowed (silt and sand-filled) to rooted. Burrowing increases upwards. Minor ripples.

UNIT 1A 3.7' 4323.0'-26.7' SHALLOW BAY TO LAGOON. Shale, laminated to rippled, burrow-mottled, interbedded with minor siltstone (15%) and sandstone (5%).

Fig. 22. Core description of the Midwest Taack No. 11 in Bell Creek Field. Note parallel-laminated sandstones interpreted as washover deposits interbedded with finer grained tidal flat and lagoonal deposits. Three thin sandstones at 4310.0 to 4312.0 ft. are interbedded with rooted to burrowed sediments (from Jordan et al, 1981).

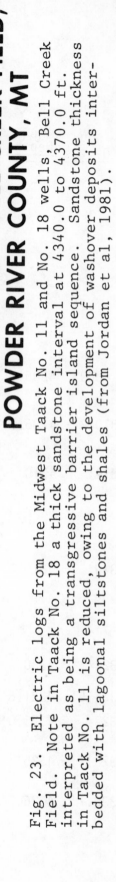

RESISTIVITY

SPONTANEOUS-POTENTIAL

CORED INTERVAL

4300

4400

MIDWEST TAACK NO. 11
NW,SE 14-9S-53E BELL CREEK FIELD,
POWDER RIVER COUNTY, MT

MUDDY FORMATION

CORED INTERVAL

4300

4400

MIDWEST TAACK NO. 18
SE,NE 13-9S-53E BELL CREEK FIELD,
POWDER RIVER COUNTY, MT

Fig. 23. Electric logs from the Midwest Taack No. 11 and No. 18 wells, Bell Creek Field. Note in Taack No. 18 a thick sandstone interval at 4340.0 to 4370.0 ft. interpreted as being a transgressive barrier island sequence. Sandstone thickness in Taack No. 11 is reduced, owing to the development of washover deposits inter- bedded with lagoonal siltstones and shales (from Jordan et al, 1981).

-36-

A similar sequence of washover deposits is found in the Taack No. 11 core, although the barrier island sequence does not appear to be as well-developed (Fig. 22). Bay, lagoon, and tidal flat shales, siltstones, and sandstones from the base of the core contain burrows, ripples, and some roots. Thin washover sandstones are overlain by marsh and tidal flat sandstones, siltstones, and shales.

Exploration for washover and barrier island sequences in the subsurface should include the recognition of thick sandstones having characteristic coarsening upwards sequence (barrier island) which lenses in a paleo-landward direction into sandstones with sharp bases interbedded with shale (Fig. 23). Cuttings may indicate a rapid succession of interbedded sandstone and shale, the sandstones being well-sorted and quartzose, the shale being carbonaceous. Cores would display features similar to those described above. Isopaching sandstones in a transgressive barrier island depositional system would reveal a linear trend of sand "thicks" with lobate sands (washover fans or flood-deltas) wedging into shales (lagoonal sediments) in a paleo-landward direction.

REGRESSIVE BARRIERS

Sedimentary Characterists

Primary sedimentary characteristics and major geologic features of regressive barrier sands are summarized in Fig. 24. Regressive barriers are depositional in nature and prograde seaward through time. The morphology of these barriers is characterized most commonly by a series of shore-parallel, tightly-spaced beach ridges. Vertical sedimentary sequences coarsen-upward and are generally comprised of fine-grained quartzose sand, with gradational internal contacts between depositional units (Fig. 24).

REGRESSIVE BARRIERS

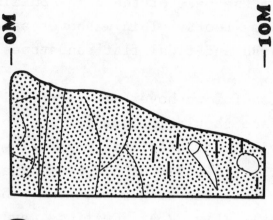

- DEPOSITIONAL (PROGRADING)
- BEACH RIDGE MORPHOLOGY
- COARSENING-UP SEQUENCE

QUARTZOSE SAND
FINE-GRAINED
GRADATIONAL CONTACTS

- MODERN ⟶ "RARE"
- ANCIENT ⟶ "COMMON"

—0M

—10M

Fig. 24. Characteristic geologic features of modern regressive (prograding) barrier island shorelines.

In modern day settings this type of sand body is relatively rare primarily as a result of Holocene eustatic sea-level rise and subsequent shoreline erosion. However, regressive barriers have been more commonly observed in ancient sequences than many other types of barrier shoreline sands. This is primarily a function of their depositional nature and therefore greater potential for preservation.

Modern Example

Kiawah and Seabrook Islands, located on the Central South Carolina coastline, are excellent examples of regressive barrier sands in a tide-dominated (mesotidal) environment (Fig. 25). The barriers are relatively wide, stunted and have a drumstick shape. Shore-parellel beach ridges dominate the island morphology and expansive salt marshes and tidal flats occur landward (Fig. 26). Tidal inlets are relatively stable in terms of lateral migration, and are associated with large ebb-tidal deltas.

Depositional Units:

Sediments comprising the barrier complex are a mixture of fossiliferous cross-bedded and burrowed sands, silts and clays. This diverse sequence of Holocene deposits can be divided into three lithologically and texturally distinct interfingering stratigraphic units or "lithosomes". These are: the barrier, back-barrier and tidal inlet. Each lithosome is comprised of a number of sedimentary depositional environments. Depositional environments were identified on the basis of texture, lithology, physical and biogenic sedimentary structures, biota and stratigraphic position. The barrier lithosome is a texturally and mineralogically uniform, coarsening upward sequence of fine-grained, well sorted sand. Representative depositional environments include the beach

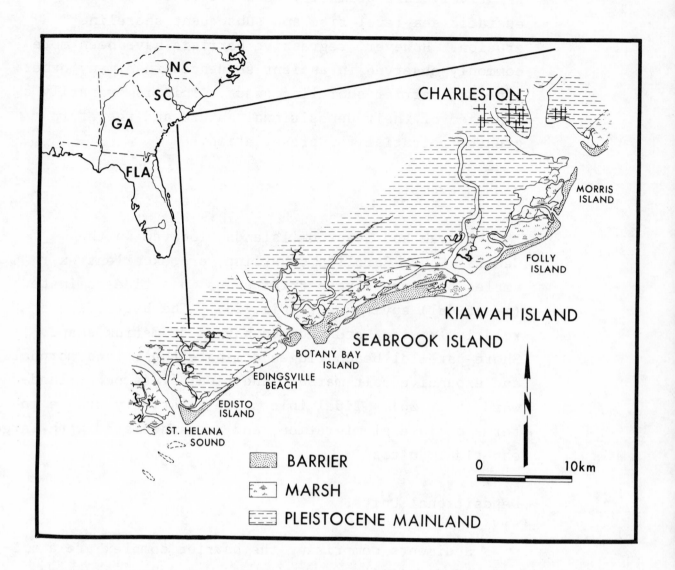

Fig. 25. Location map of Kiawah and Seabrook Islands. Both
islands are progradational beach-ridge barriers backed by
extensive salt marsh and tidal flats. Transgressive barriers
occur immediately to the north (Folly Beach and Morris Island)
and to the south (Bothany Bay Island, Edingsville Beach and
Edisto Island).

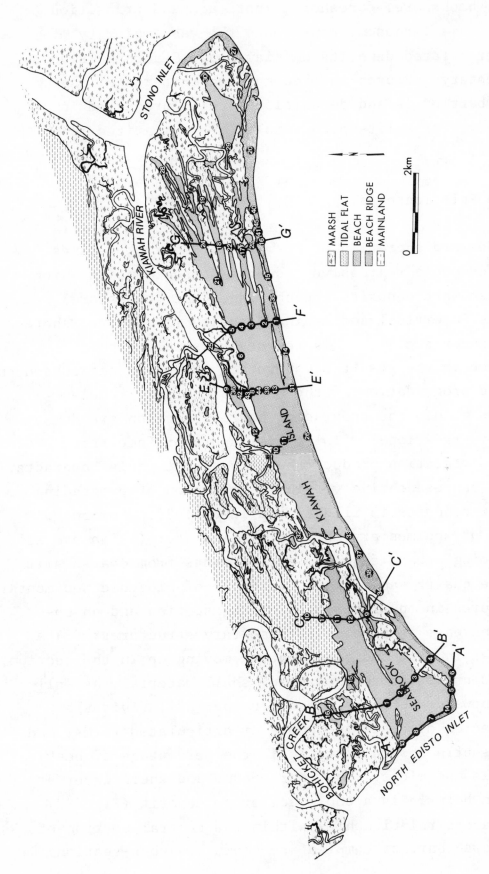

Fig. 26. Geomorphology map of a prograding barrier island system of the central South Carolina coast (from Moslow and Colquhoun, 1981).

ridge, backshore, foreshore, shoreface and transition zone. This lithosome represents the vast majority of barrier-related deposits on Kiawah and Seabrook Islands. Sedimentary features and recognition criteria of the major barrier island depositional units preserved in vibracores or split-spoon samples are summarized in Table 2.

Facies Relationships:

Seaward accretion of Kiawah and Seabrook Islands has produced a regressive sequence of sediment in which more landward deposits (beach-ridge/dune, backshore) overlie intertidal and marine deposits (foreshore, shoreface, inner shelf). This regressive stratigraphic sequence is the result of shoreface accretion and subsequent seaward progradation of the barrier complex. Facies changes within the prograding barrier section are dominantly gradational. Inlet-fill and shoreface storm lag sedimentation produce the only abrupt facies contacts.

A representative vertical succession of prograding barrier deposits is illustrated in Fig. 27. Common trends of sedimentary characteristics are: (1) an overall coarsening-upward sequence of sediments from coarse silt to fine quartz sand; (2) a dominance of biogenic sedimentary structures in the lower half of the section and an upward increase in physical sedimentary structures; (3) a decrease in silt and clay content moving up in the section; (4) a decrease in the amount of shell material, as well as an upward decrease in size, number of individuals and species diversity of whole or articulated forms; and (5) a subtle upward decrease in the percentage of heavy minerals and micas. The coarse sand and shell layer at -8 m in hole 16 is a shoreface storm deposit (Fig. 27).

Facies relationships within the central portion of the Kiawah barrier complex are shown in cross-section

Table 2. Sedimentary Characteristics and Recognition Criteria in Cores of Prograding Barrier Depositional Units

Unit	Biota	Holocene Barrier Texture/Lithology	Sedimentary Structures
Beach ridge dune	Uniola paniculata; shells leached	Fine to very fine, clean, well-sorted, quartz sand	Trough and planar cross-bedding; rooted, burrowed
Backshore	Uniola paniculata; rafted Spartina sp.	Fine, well-sorted, clean quartz sand	Low angle planar cross-bedding; rooted; flat beds of heavy minerals
Foreshore to upper shoreface	Rare Donax sp. and Mulinia sp. fragments	Very fine, very well-sorted, clean quartz sand	Low angle planar and trough cross-bedding; antidune bedding
Mid-lower shoreface	Mulinia lateralis; Donax variabilis; Spisula solidissima	Very fine, well-sorted slightly silty quartz sand	Laminae sets of silty clay; moderate burrowing (Callianassa major)
Transition zone to offshore	Mulinia lateralis; Spisula solidissima; Andara sp.; Epitonium sp.	Very fine, moderately well-sorted silty quartz sand and shell	Interbedded layers of silty sand and silty clay; rare laminae of silty sand; extensive burrowing (Callianassa biformis)

PROGRADING BARRIER SEQUENCE
KI-16

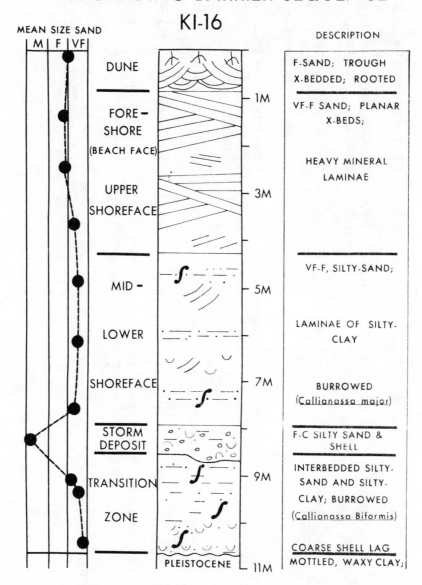

Fig. 27. Vertical sequence of sediments from core hole KI-16 on Kiawah Island. A description of primary sedimentary structures and textures for each Holocene barrier unit is given in the right hand column. Mean grain size is shown on the left. An overall coarsening-upward trend in grain size and an upward increase in preserved physical sedimentary structures are observed.

F-F' (Fig. 28). The transect is developed across a series of tightly-welded Holocene beach ridges with intermittent swales (Fig. 26).

In cross-section F-F', a wedge-shaped sand body geometry is observed for the Holocene barrier lithosome (Fig. 28). Shoreface and foreshore deposits dominate the seaward-thickening Holocene section, pinching out or abutting against a back-barrier sequence 1.5 km landward of the present shoreline. The Holocene stratigraphy is capped by a fine-grained sand beach-ridge and backshore sequence. Inner-shelf sediments underlie shoreface deposits at the base of the pro-grading barrier sequence (Fig. 28). The majority of the island complex is composed of a relatively thick (8.0-10.0 m) prograding (regressive) sequence of barrier sands that interfinger with offshore silts and clays.

Recognition and Preservation:

Because of their depositional nature and association with high rates of sand accumulation, regressive barriers have a much greater potential for preservation in ancient sequences. The upper portion of the prograding barrier sequence has a very low potential for preservation. Mean-dering tidal creeks and laterally migrating tidal inlets erode or rework beach ridge, foreshore and upper shoreface deposits. The tidal creek channel-fill and inlet-fill deposits, on the other hand, have a much greater chance for preservation. With continued high sediment supply, low wave energy and relatively stable sea level, the lower two-thirds of the prograding barrier sequence (mid-lower shoreface, transition zone) have an excellent potential for being preserved.

In opposition to the transgressive type of barrier island, regressive barriers have a much greater potential

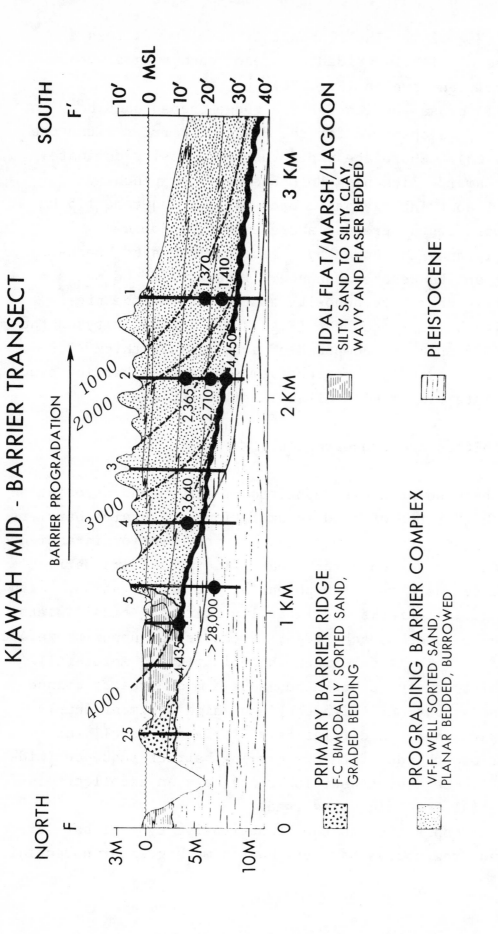

Fig. 28. Generalized cross section through the mid-barrier portion of Kiawah Island showing the main stratigraphic components of the prograding (regressive) barrier island complex (from Moslow, 1980).

as subsurface hydrocarbon reservoirs. Regressive barriers are thicker, more homogeneous, and more continuous along strike and dip. These subsurface characteristics are shown in the three dimensional block diagram of Kiawah Island (Fig. 29). This type of barrier sand could serve as an excellent stratigraphic trap. Up-dip salt marsh muds and down-dip offshore silts and clays could serve as potential seal and/or source beds.

Stratigraphic models of sand body geometry and characteristic log response for regressive barriers in wave and tide dominated settings are shown in Fig. 30. Regressive barrier sands are relatively thick and laterally continuous along strike. Sand body geometry is wedge-shaped along dip. Barrier sands pinch out or abut back-barrier muds up-dip, and grade into offshore silts and clays down-dip. Gamma-ray and resistivity log response shows an increase in sand content and porosity towards the top of the sequence (Fig. 30).

Ancient Example

The Crestaceous-aged Fox Hills Sandstone of Colorado and Wyoming has been interpreted as a prograding marine shoreline sand (Land, 1972; Weimer and Tillman, 1980). Portions of the Fox Hills sandstone have many affinities to regressive barrier islands. A paleogeographic map of the Western Interior Seaway during late Fox Hills deposition shows the irregular orientation and configuration of this marine shoreline sand (Fig. 31). Regressive barrier sands should be found along this trend within the embayments of the shoreline where tidal range is amplified and barrier island formation more likely.

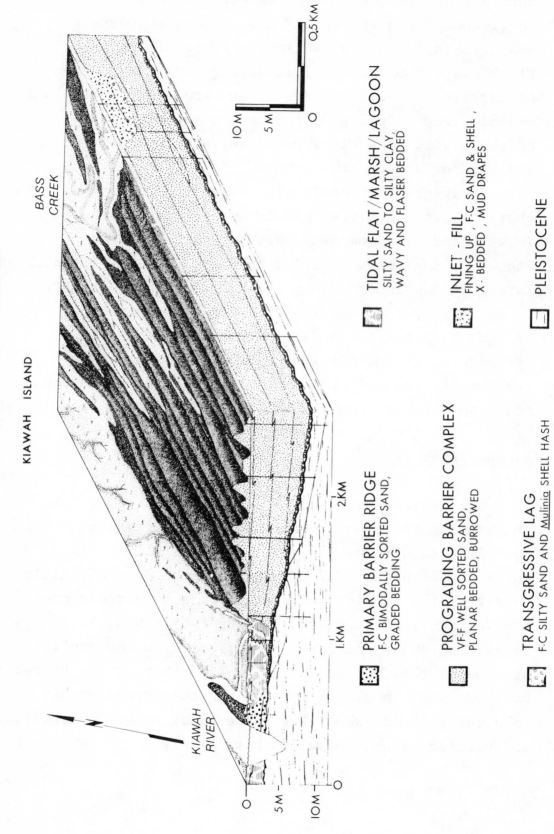

PROGRADING MESOTIDAL BARRIER COMPLEX

KIAWAH ISLAND

BASS CREEK

KIAWAH RIVER

TIDAL FLAT/MARSH/LAGOON
SILTY SAND TO SILTY CLAY,
WAVY AND FLASER BEDDED

INLET - FILL
FINING UP, F-C SAND & SHELL,
X - BEDDED, MUD DRAPES

PLEISTOCENE

PRIMARY BARRIER RIDGE
F-C BIMODALLY SORTED SAND,
GRADED BEDDING

PROGRADING BARRIER COMPLEX
VF-F WELL SORTED SAND,
PLANAR BEDDED, BURROWED

TRANSGRESSIVE LAG
F-C SILTY SAND AND Mulinia SHELL HASH

0.5 KM

10 M
5 M
0

Fig. 29. Diagram displaying Holocene facies relationships along dip and strike sections in the mid and updrift portions of Kiawah Island. A similar geometry and stratigraphy should be found in most prograding barrier islands (from Moslow, 1980).

-48-

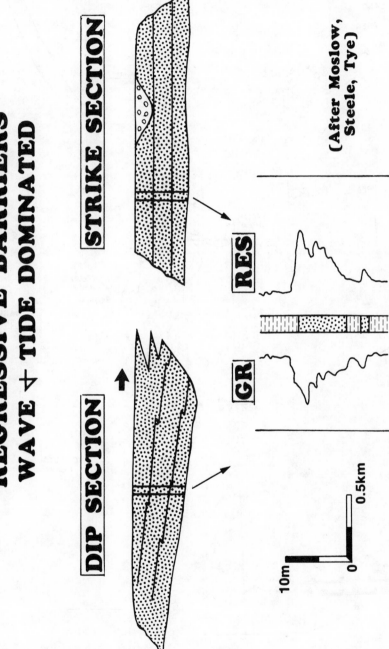

Fig. 30. Sand body geometry and characteristic log response for regressive barrier shorelines.

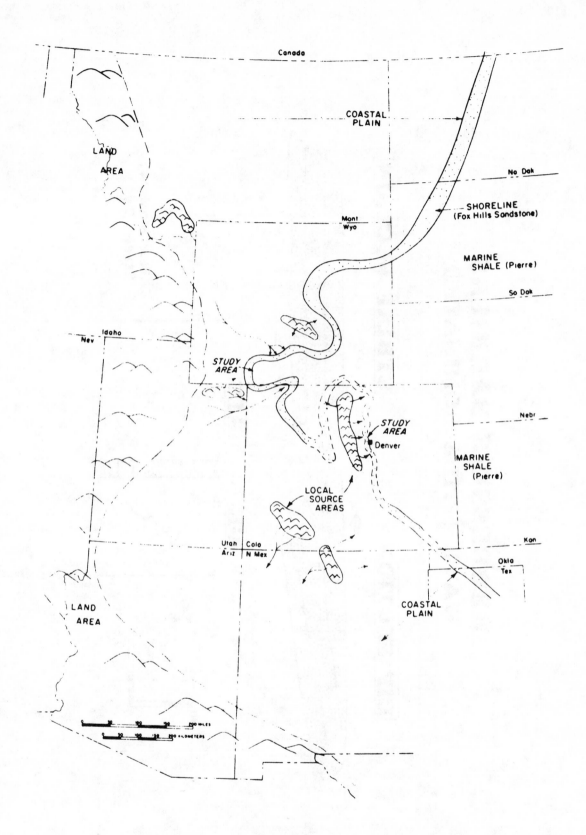

Fig. 31. Regional index map and paleogeography of
western interior, U.S., during late Fox Hills deposition.
Front Range uplift is indicated as shedding sediment into
the Pierre Sea (from Weimer and Tillman, 1980).

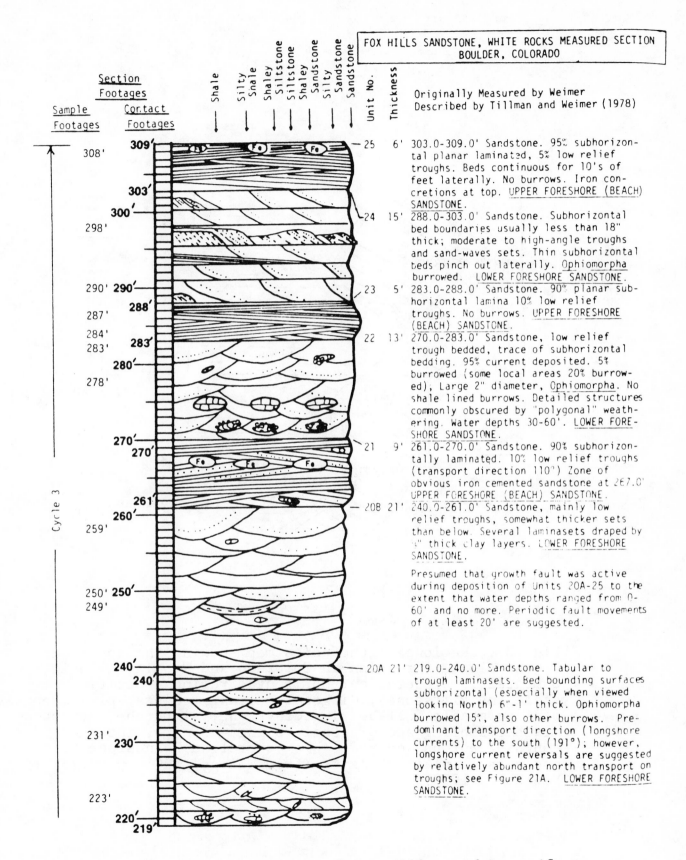

Section
Footages

Sample
Footages

Contact
Footages

Shale
Silty Shale
Shaley Siltstone
Siltstone
Shaley Sandstone
Silty Sandstone
Sandstone

Unit No.

Thickness

Originally Measured by Weimer
Described by Tillman and Weimer (1978)

25 6' 303.0-309.0' Sandstone. 95% subhorizontal planar laminated, 5% low relief troughs. Beds continuous for 10's of feet laterally. No burrows. Iron concretions at top. UPPER FORESHORE (BEACH) SANDSTONE.

24 15' 288.0-303.0' Sandstone. Subhorizontal bed boundaries usually less than 18" thick; moderate to high-angle troughs and sand-waves sets. Thin subhorizontal beds pinch out laterally. Ophiomorpha burrowed. LOWER FORESHORE SANDSTONE.

23 5' 283.0-288.0' Sandstone. 90% planar subhorizontal lamina 10% low relief troughs. No burrows. UPPER FORESHORE (BEACH) SANDSTONE.

22 13' 270.0-283.0' Sandstone, low relief trough bedded, trace of subhorizontal bedding. 95% current deposited. 5% burrowed (some local areas 20% burrowed), Large 2" diameter, Ophiomorpha. No shale lined burrows. Detailed structures commonly obscured by "polygonal" weathering. Water depths 30-60'. LOWER FORESHORE SANDSTONE.

21 9' 261.0-270.0' Sandstone. 90% subhorizontally laminated. 10% low relief troughs (transport direction 110°) Zone of obvious iron cemented sandstone at 267.0' UPPER FORESHORE (BEACH) SANDSTONE.

20B 21' 240.0-261.0' Sandstone, mainly low relief troughs, somewhat thicker sets than below. Several laminasets draped by ¾" thick clay layers. LOWER FORESHORE SANDSTONE.

Presumed that growth fault was active during deposition of Units 20A-25 to the extent that water depths ranged from 0-60' and no more. Periodic fault movements of at least 20' are suggested.

20A 21' 219.0-240.0' Sandstone. Tabular to trough laminasets. Bed bounding surfaces subhorizontal (especially when viewed looking North) 6"-1' thick. Ophiomorpha burrowed 15%, also other burrows. Predominant transport direction (longshore currents) to the south (191°); however, longshore current reversals are suggested by relatively abundant north transport on troughs; see Figure 21A. LOWER FORESHORE SANDSTONE.

Cycle 3

Fig. 32. Outcrop section of Fox Hills sandstone (from Weimer and Tillman, 1980).

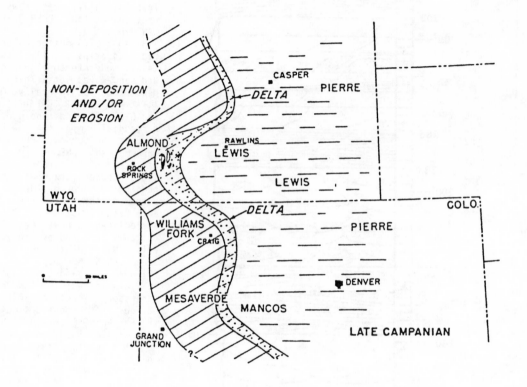

Fig. 33. Regional lithofacies map showing the upper part
of the Almond formation in Colorado and Wyoming. Environmental interpretation: horizontal ruling = neritic
shale and siltstones; diagonal ruling = coastal-plain deposits
of impermeable coal-bearing claystone, siltstone, sandstone;
mixed stippling and diagonal ruling = zone of inter-
tonguing porous and permeable (shoreline) sandstone beds
and coastal-plain deposits (from Weimer, 1966, p. 2173; in
Van Horn, 1979).

Wiemer and Tillman (1980) described outcrop
sections of the Fox Hills Sandstone that are similar
to the regressive shoreface sequences associated with
modern prograding barrier islands (Fig. 32). Cross-
bedded and burrowed lower and upper foreshore sandstones of the Fox Hills are almost identical in
terms of sedimentary characteristics to the foreshore and shoreface sands of Kiawah Island, South
Carolina, a modern regressive barrier island (Figs.
27 and 32).

An excellent ancient example of a regressive
barrier island sandstone that occurs as a subsurface
hydrocarbon reservoir, is the Almond Formation in
the Patrick Draw Field of Wyoming. A generalized
regional lithofacies map showing paleoenvironments
during time of deposition for the Creataceous aged
Almond Formation is shown in Figure 33.

The Almond Formation in the Patrick Draw Field
is discussed in detail as an ancient barrier island
sand in the next section on tidal inlet depositional
systems.

TIDAL INLETS

Before leaving barrier island shoreline depositional systems, a very important sedimentary environment, the tidal inlet, must be examined. The channel
sands and tidal deltas associated with the inlet environment are geologically most important. Tidal inlets
can migrate laterally along a shoreline reworking the
previously deposited barrier island sediments, and
deposit thick sequences of fining upward inlet-fill.
Recent studies have shown that as much as 50% of the
sediment associated with a modern barrier shoreline is

deposited in the inlet environment (Moslow and Tye, 1984).

Sedimentary Characteristics

Variations in the Sedimentary characteristics of tidal inlet deposits is primarily a function of the inverse relationship between wave height and tidal range. However, in addition to hydrographic regime (waves, tides and storms), sediment supply (quanity and lithology), and the pre-Holocene substrate (topographic relief and lithology) modify tidal inlet distribution, geometries and sequences. The geologic controls on tidal inlet stratigraphy and an overview of the varying types of inlet sequences in wave vs. tide dominated environments are shown in Fig. 34.

Shore-parallel lateral migration of tidal inlet channels significantly reworks adjacent barrier islands coarsening upward shoreface sequences, commonly associated with prograding (regressive) barriers, and coarsening-upward washover-lagoon sequences associated with landward-migrating (transgressive) barriers, are commonly replaced by fining-upward tidal inlet sequences. Tidal inlet sedimentary sequences can display numerous subtle to strikingly dramatic variations in shore-parallel (strike) and shore-perpendicular (dip) directions.

Modern Example

Depositional models for wave-dominated (mircotidal) and tide-dominated (mesotidal) inlets are best observed along the North Carolina/South Carolina coasts. These study sites were introduced previously in the sections

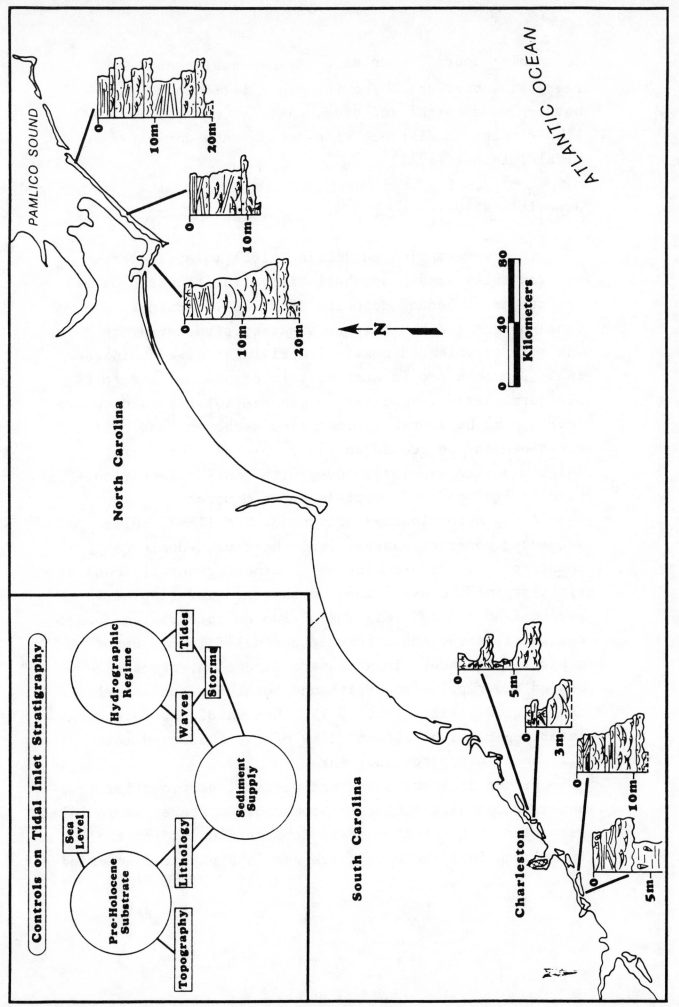

Fig. 34. Diagram showing the controls on tidal inlet stratigraphy and variations in sedimentary sequences in wave and tide dominated environments. (from Tye & Moslow, in press)

concerning modern examples of transgressive and regressive barriers. The inverse relationship between wave height and tidal range along this coastline results in distinct tide-versus wave-dominated tidal inlets (Fig. 35).

Depositional Units:

In a wave-dominated setting tidal inlet sequences are generally sand- and shell-rich, fine-to very coarse grained cross-bedded deposits (Fig. 36). Grain size fines-upward and biogenic sedimentary structures are rare. The most prevalent deposits comprising a wave-dominated inlet sequence are inlet floor, inlet channel and spit platform. Seawardmost wave-dominated inlet sequences are overlain by horizontally laminated washover sand and/or cross-bedded and rooted eolian dune sand. Landward, inlet deposits are interbedded with fine-grained flood-tidal delta sand and overlain by salt marsh.

Along more tidally-influenced shorelines, inlet sequences contrast sharply from their wave-dominated counterparts. Tide-dominated sequences generally consist of finer-grained, cross-bedded to burrowed and rippled interbedded sand and mud (Fig. 37). Two or more fining-upward cycles of active and abandoned channel-fill may comprise a single sequence. In a seaward direction, cross-bedded and rippled ebb-delta and foreshore sand overlies the inlet deposits (Tye, 1984). Landward, the foreshore interfingers with silt and clay of the abandoned inlet-fill and bioturbated salt marsh.

Figure 38 shows idealized vertical sections for tide- and wave-dominated inlets. Geomorphic differences in inlet formation, migration, and abandonment account for the variations in lithology, thickness, and physical and biogenic

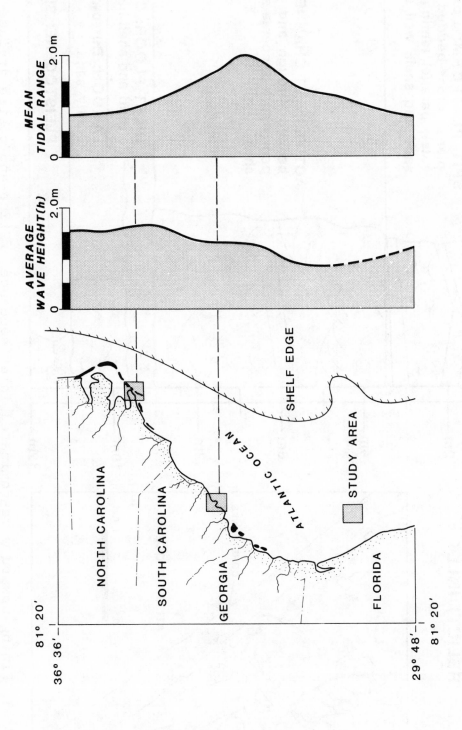

Fig. 35. Diagram showing the inverse relationship between wave height and tidal range along the southeastern United States. (from Tye and Moslow, in press).

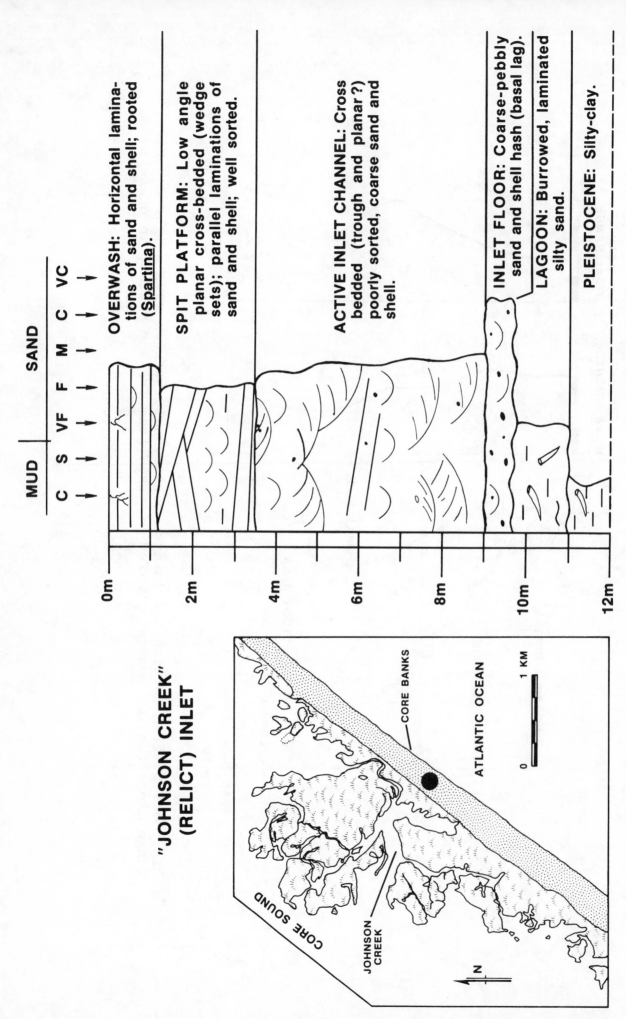

Fig. 36. Fining-upward wave-dominated inlet sequence of fine-and coarse-grained, cross-bedded sand and shell. This sequence was deposited by the lateral migration of a formerly active inlet in the vicinity of Johnson Creek, Core Banks, North Carolina (see inset) (From Moslow and Tye, 1984).

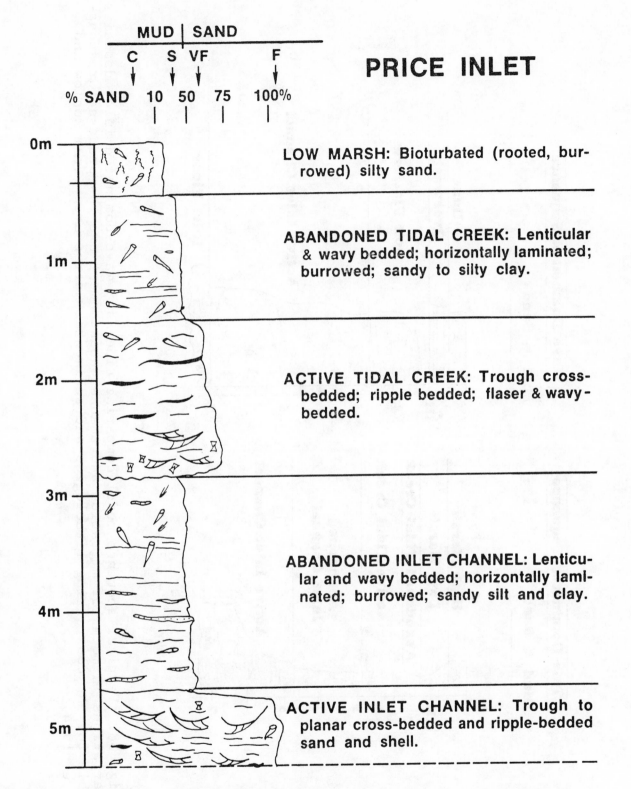

Fig. 37. Characteristic tide-dominated (mesotidal) inlet sequence from the central South Carolina coast (from Moslow and Tye, 1984; and Tye, 1984).

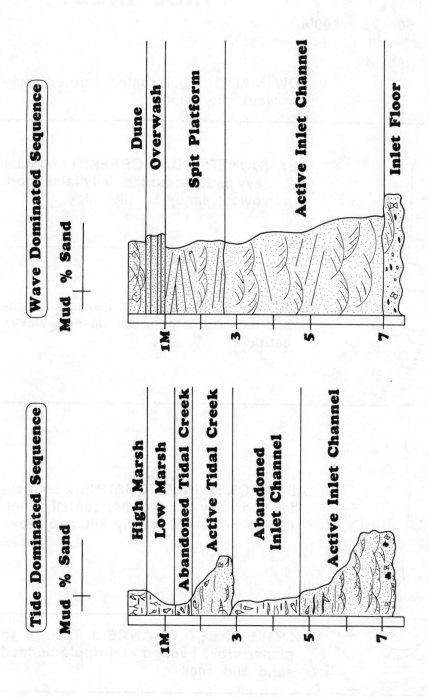

Fig. 38. Vertical sequence model comparing tide- and wave-dominated inlet deposits. Variations in modes of migration and channel abandonment are the processes responsible for the contrasting lithologies and sedimentary structures (from Moslow and Tye, 1984).

sedimentary structures. Planar and trough cross-bedded medium- to fine-grained sands form thick, fining-upward deposits in wave-dominated inlets. Tide-dominated inlet sequences fine-upward from medium- to fine-grained sand into silt and clay in the abandoned channel plug. Most of the primary structures are destroyed by burrowing and rooting during channel abandonment.

Facies Relationships:

Cross-sections across abandoned wave-dominated inlet channels are lenticular to wedge-shaped when viewed along depositional strike (Fig. 39). Active and relict channels display obvious cutbank (erosional) and accretional margins, revealing the direction of migration. An associated recurved spit comprises the accreting margin and fills the inlet channel as it migrates.

Once abandoned, the channel-fill deposited in shallow wave-dominated inlets is lenticular in cross-section. Rapid channel migration and high sediment supply result in thin, laterally continuous sequences of inlet-deposited sediment (Captain Sam's and Old Drum Inlet: Fig. 39). Deeper tidal inlets, entrenched in Pleistocene "basement" are generally less laterally extensive and display wedge-shaped strike-oriented geometries (Swash Inlet and Johnson Creek: Fig 39). Thickness to width ratios reflecting maximum scour depth and lateral migration, range from 1:150 for deep channels, to 1:500 for shallower channels. The high ratio for shallow tidal inlets is due to the absence of paleotopographic control, rapid downdrift migration and a small tidal prism.

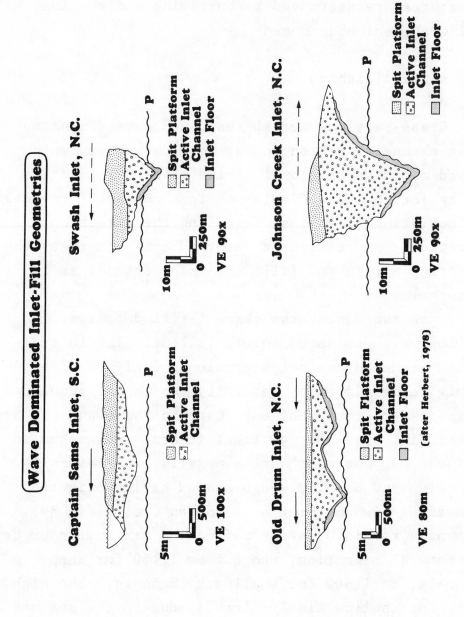

Fig. 39. Wave-dominated inlet sand body geometries and facies relationships.

Greater channel scour and Pleistocene control
at Johnson Creek (Fig. 36) limited channel migration
and produced a V-shaped inlet channel deposit (Fig. 40).
Channel confinement by Pleistocene sediments resulted
in a 9.5 m thick wedge of fining-upward deposits preserved
within Core Banks. Herbert (1978) described an inlet
sequence of similar geometry on Portsmouth Island, North
Carolina; however, he observed four separate fining-
upward cycles of inlet deposition. Inlet deposits may
be stacked by sea level rise, barrier island subsidence
or by successively filling the thalweg of an old fluvial
channel (Price and Parker, 1981). The depositon of four
stacked sequences indicates that sea-level rise or land
subsidence was rapid enough to displace the previously
deposited sediment and prevent it from being reworked.
Inlet channel stability may account for only one channel
sequence at Johnson Creek, but more likely, the earlier
deposits were reworked by successive episodes of tidal
inlet migration.

Tide-dominated channels along South Carolina
coast are confined in the Pleistocene substrate and
exhibit symmetrical U-shaped strike-oriented geometries
(Fig. 41.). Inlet throat stability and bar-bypassing
at the channel mouth inhibit extensive lateral migration
and thus tidal inlet deposits accumulate in the updrift
portion of barrier islands (Fig. 42). The strike-oriented
cross-section at Price Inlet (Capers Island) illustrates
the U-shaped inlet and the preservation of a concave-
upward wedge of inlet-channel sand overlain by fine-
grained abandoned-channel deposits (Fig. 42). Compared
to wave-dominated inlets, more time is required to totally
close and fill an abandoned tide-dominated inlet channel.
Inlet closure by a landward migrating swash bar restricts

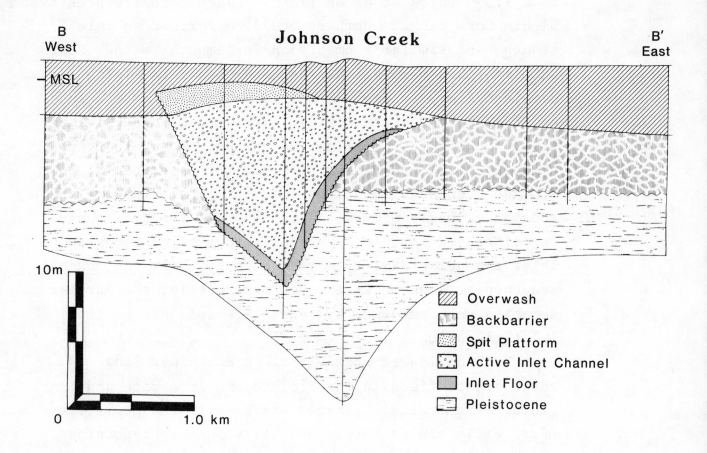

Fig. 40. Strike-oriented (shore parallel) cross-section of a wave-dominated inlet-fill at Johnson Creek, Core Banks, North Carolina (after Moslow and Heron, 1978).

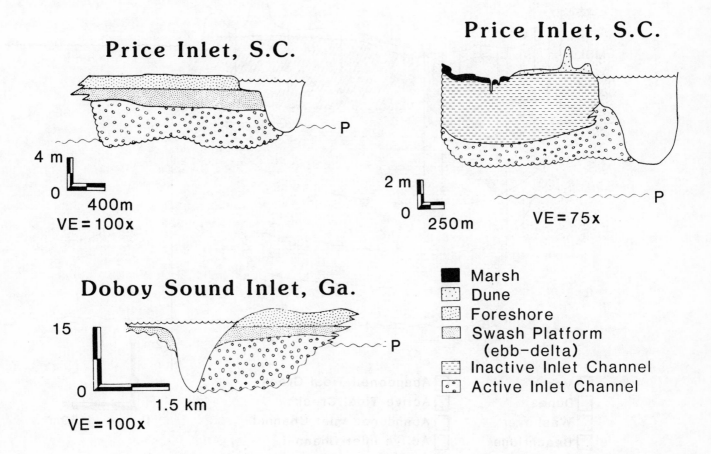

Price Inlet, S.C.

Price Inlet, S.C.

Doboy Sound Inlet, Ga.

Marsh
Dune
Foreshore
Swash Platform
(ebb-delta)
Inactive Inlet Channel
Active Inlet Channel

Fig. 41. Tide-dominated inlet sand body geometries and facies relationships (from Tye and Moslow, in press).

Price Inlet

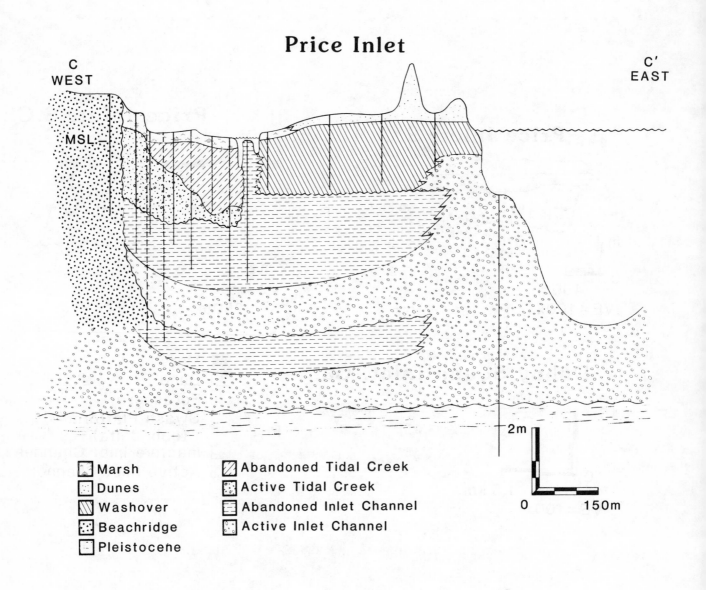

Fig. 42. Strike-oriented (shore-parallel) cross-section of a tide-dominated inlet-fill at Price Inlet, South Carolina (from Tye, 1984).

current energy in the former channel and initiates
the deposition of a fine-grained abandoned channel-
fill plug. Inlet deposits thin toward the former
inlet margins and are separated from the barrier
island by scour contacts (Fig. 42).

Recognition and Preservation:

One of the more striking recognition criteria
of wave-dominated inlet sequences is the characteristic
wedge or V-shaped shore-parallel sand body geometry
(Fig. 42). This is a function of preservation of the
downdrift cutbank and the associated accretional channel
margin.

Active inlet deposits typically thin towards the
channel margins and are scoured into barrier island
sand. Along depositional dip, sandy wave-dominated
inlets interfinger seaward with poorly developed ebb-
tidal deltas and fine-grained transitional to shelf
deposits (Fig. 43). Landward, these inlet channels
scour and interfinger with large flood-tidal deltas
and lagoonal sediments (Barwis and Hayes, 1978;
Berelson, 1979).

Tide-dominated inlets continuously migrate within
a restricted zone and create U-shaped (strike) and
crescentric concave-upward (dip) channel geometries
(Fig. 44). Mud-filled tide-dominated inlet channels
interfinger seaward (down-dip) with foreshore and ebb-tidal
delta sands. The active inlet-fill extends landward (up-dip)
into the saltmarsh and abandoned inlet-fill interfingers
with salt marsh and tidal creek deposits (Fig. 44). Clay
plugs in these abandoned channels separate barrier island
sands along strike and create a localized impermeable

INLET SEQUENCES
WAVE-DOMINATED

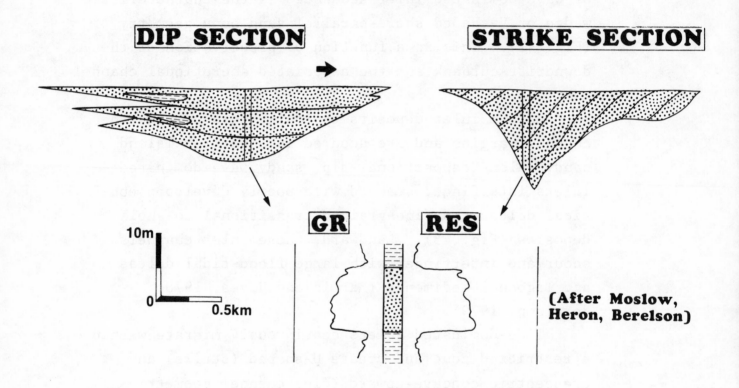

Fig. 43. Sand body geometry and characteristic log response
for wave-dominated inlet deposits (from Tye and Moslow, in press).

-68-

INLET SEQUENCES
TIDE-DOMINATED

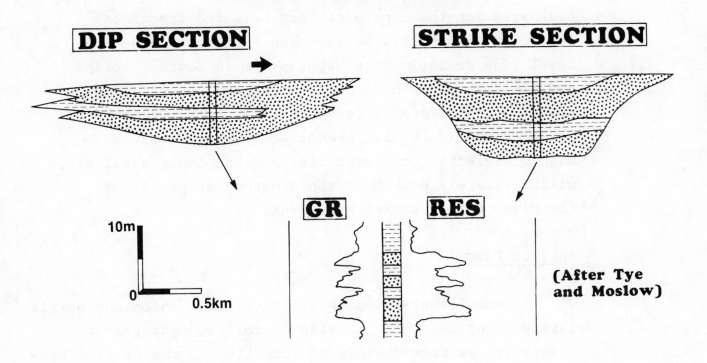

Fig. 44. Sand-body geometry and log response for tide-dominated inlet deposits (from Tye and Moslow, in press).

boundary between the ebb-tidal delta, barrier island, and back-barrier tidal creeks. The interbedded nature of impermeable muds and more permeable sands in the tide-dominated inlet sequences is reflected in the hypothetical gamma ray and resistivity log responses shown in Fig. 44.

Due to the tidal inlets stratigraphic position and the occasional occurrance of overlying and underlying fine-grained sediments, tidal inlets are the most pre-servable portion of the barrier lithosome. Thus, during transgression the uppermost foreshore and shoreface sediments will likely be reworked. If during one sea-level rise scenario, the upper 6-8 m in South Carolina and 10-12 m in North Carolina is eroded, only a thin veneer of shoreface sands separating laterally abundant 3-4 m thick tidal inlet channels will be preserved. Rate of relative sea-level rise and the inner shelf slope will ultimately determine the sequence of preserved shoreline deposits (Fischer, 1961).

Ancient Example

An excellent ancient example of tidal inlet and barrier island deposits, which is also a prolific hydrocarbon reservoir, is from the Almond Formation in the Patrick Draw Field of Wyoming. The Almond Formation (upper Mesaverde Group) is part of a Cretaceous marine shoreline sandstone in the Rocky Mountain area. In one area along the western part of the Wamsutter arch of south-central Wyoming (Fig. 45), the Almond Formation contains oil and gas in two main shoreline sandstones (Weimer and Tillman, 1982). These sandstones, the UA5 and UA6, have been interpreted as tidal inlet and barrier island deposits and form stratigraphic

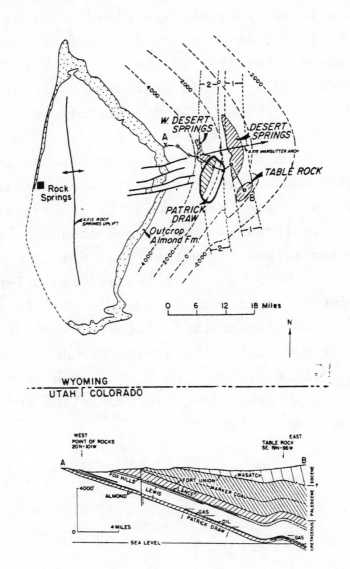

Fig. 45. Structure contour map on top of the Almond Formation (above) and structural section across the Patrick Draw Field area (from Weimer and Tillman, 1982).

traps in the Patrick Draw Field (Fig. 46). Approximately 56 million bbls of oil and 11 Bcf of gas have been produced since 1959 in the Patrick Draw Field (Weimer and Tillman 1982). It is estimated that 200 to 250 million bbls are in place in the reservoir.

The UA-6 sandstone is fine grained, calcareous ranges from 0-25 ft. in thickness, has an erratic distribution and pinches out up-dip (paleolandward) into lagoonal shale (Weimer and Tillman 1982). The UA-6 is interpreted as tidal creek channels landward of a barrier island shoreline (Fig. 47).

The UA-5 sandstone is the main oil-productive sandstone at Patrick Draw. The UA-5 is quartzose, fine-to medium-grained, calcareous and displays both fining and coarsening upward trends. Weimer and Tillman, (1982) interpret the UA-5 sandstone as having been deposited in prograding barrier island and tidal inlet environments (Fig. 47).

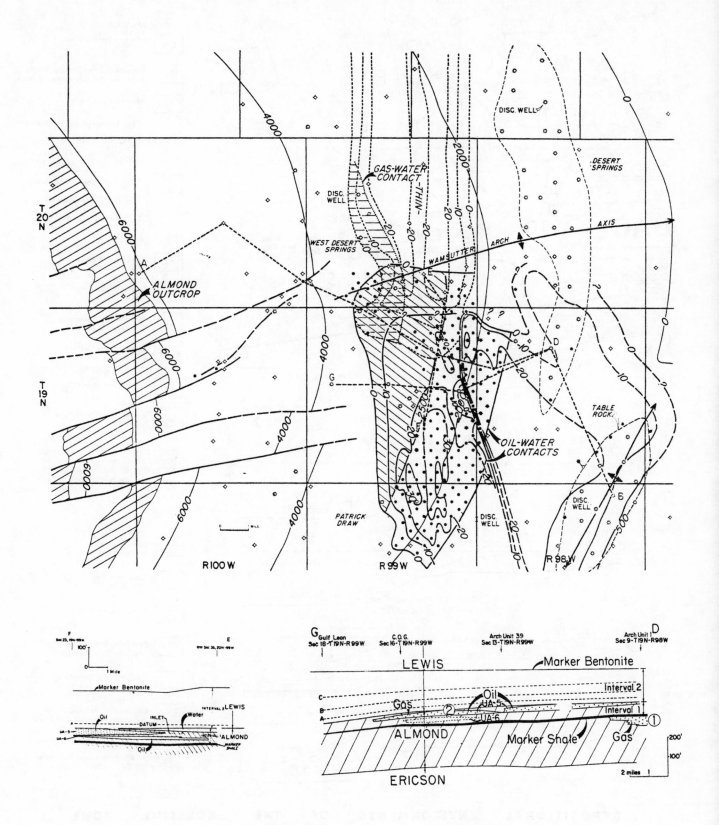

Fig. 46. Isopach map of the UA-5 sandstone in the Patrick Draw Field with stratigraphic cross-sections. Contour interval is 10 ft. (from Weimer and Tillman, 1982).

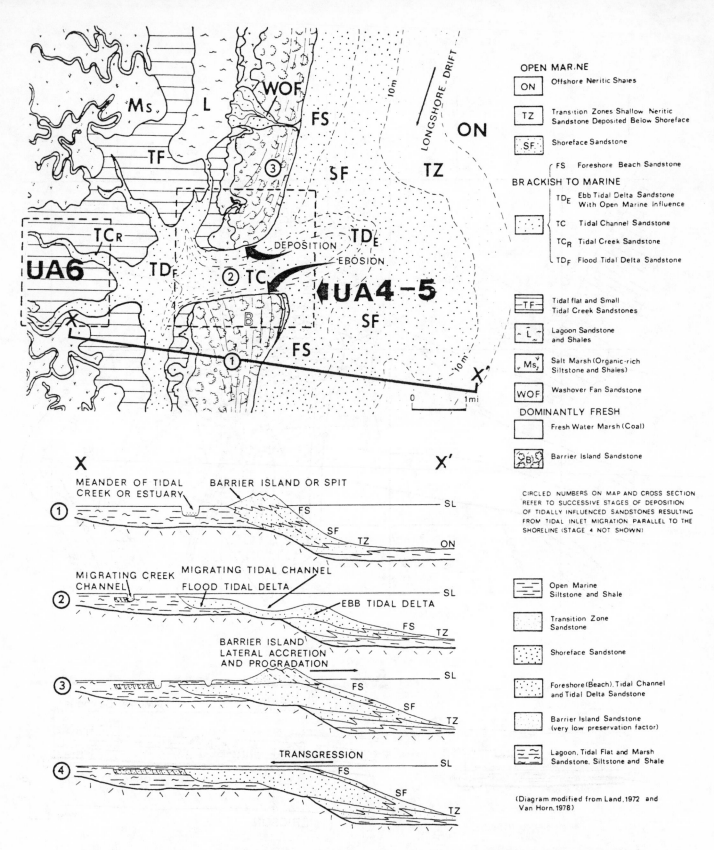

DEPOSITIONAL ENVIRONMENTS OF THE SHORELINE ZONE

Fig. 47. Depositional environments of the shoreline zone summarized from modern environments and modified to represent stratigraphic model for petroleum-productive Almond sandstones. UA6 sandstone at West Desert Springs is believed representative of tidal channel, tidal creeks, and lower tidal sand flats inland from main shoreline zone. UA4 and UA5 sandstones are tidal channels of main shoreline sand zone (from Weimer et al, 1982).

SHOREFACE AND INNER SHELF SYSTEMS

Introduction

For the purposes of these notes, sand deposits associated with shoreface and inner-continental shelf depositional systems are categorized into three types. This categorization is related to processes (i.e. waves, tides, storms and deltaic influence) and is as follows:

1) shoreface and shelf sand ridges and shoal massifs in wave and storm-dominated settings. The best known examples of these types of sand bodies are from the eastern seaboard of the United States (Fig. 48).

2) sand ridges in tide-dominated settings. These are more commonly referred to as tidal ridges and are found in some estuarine and shelf environments (Fig. 49).

3) submerged inner-continental shelf sand shoals in deltaic settings. Excellent examples of these types of sand shoals are found on the Louisiana continental shelf in the Gulf of Mexico (Fig. 50).

Controls on Sedimentation and Stratigraphy

The stratigraphy and evolution of shoreface and inner-shelf sand bodies is dependent on several geologic parameters. Among these are the following:

1) Hydrographic Regime (waves, storms and tides)
2) Shoreface Retreat (rate and extent of shoreface erosion)
3) Fluvial and Deltaic Input (sediment source and supply)

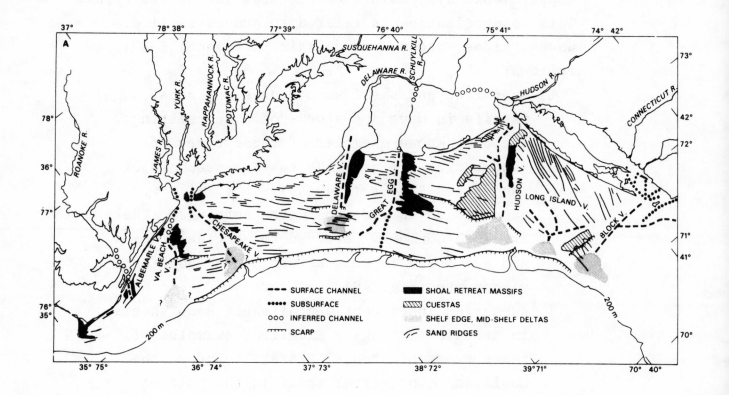

Fig. 48. Major morphological features of the Middle Atlantic
Bight. Note relationship of shoal retreat massifs to present
estuaries, and to capes (e.g. Cape Hatteras, lower left corner
of diagram) and consistent angle of linear sand ridges to shoreline (average 22°). (From Johnson, 1978; after Swift et al.,
1973; in Walker, 1979).

-76-

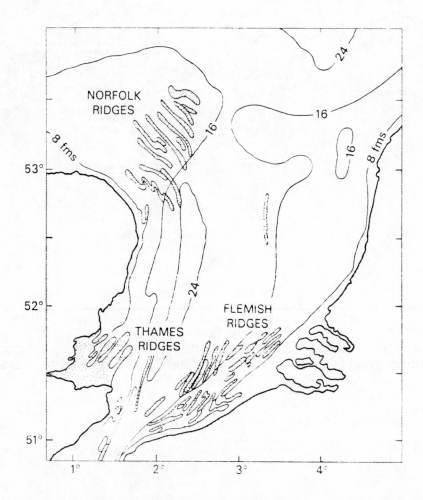

Fig. 49. The main fields of tidal sand ridges in the
Southern North Sea (after Houbolt, 1968; in Johnson, 1978).

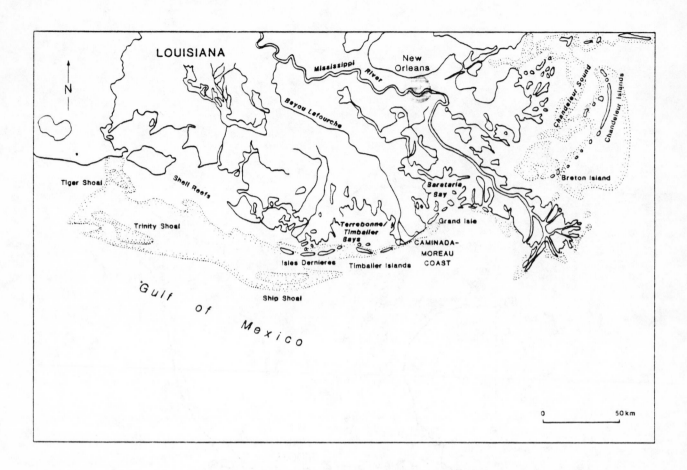

Fig. 50. Sand distribution patterns on the Louisiana
inner shelf and shoreface (Penland and Boyd, in press).

4) Antecedent Topography, and

5) Basin subsidence and sea-level rise (submergence and preservation.

Penland and Boyd (1981) and Penland et al (1981) have
provided an evolutionary model for inner shelf shoals
that also displays the interrelationship between deltaic
headland, barrier island shorelines and shoreface
and shelf sand bodies (Fig. 51).

SHOAL MASSIFS

Shoal massifs are cape-associated sand ridges
that are shore-normal to shore-oblique and extend
from the shoreline to the seaward limit of the continental shelf. These sand shoals are extremely large
subaqueous features and form sites of littoral drift
covergence, thereby serving as sediment sinks. Best
examples of shoal massifs are from the eastern United
States continental shelf where Cape Hatteras, Lookout,
Fear and Romain are each associated with a large sand
shoal (Fig. 52).

Sedimentary Characteristics

The origin of capes and shoals along the U.S. east
coast, like the origin of barrier islands, has long been
a subject of controversy. While no one mechanism can
explain the development of capes and shoals around the
world's coastlines, neither is there one dominant mode
of formation for these capes along the southeastern
coast of the United States. It is most likely, that
the large shoal massifs and capes of the eastern United
States have formed as a result of antecedant topography
or the erosional retreat of deltaic headlands or a com-
bination of both.

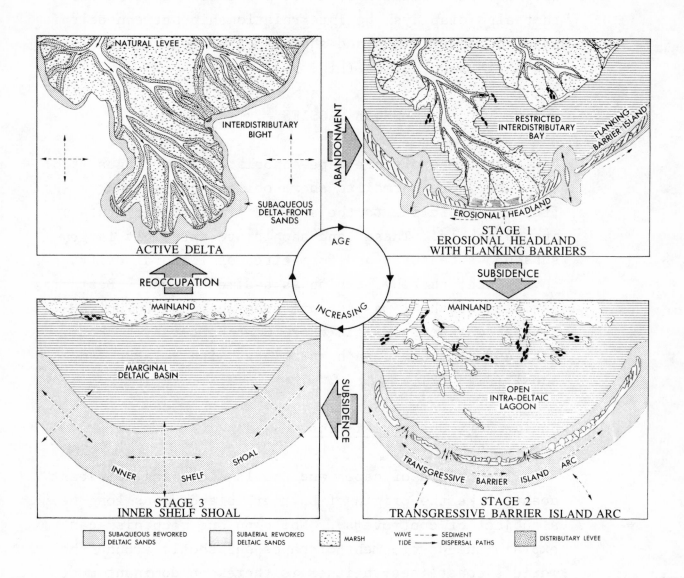

Fig. 51. An evolutionary model for deltaic barrier
development (Penland et al., 1981)

Modern Example

Sedimentologic and stratigraphic data exists for a cape-shoal complex at Cape Lookout, North Carolina (Figs. 52 and 53). Sedimentary processes and shoreline evolution for this area were discussed in the previous section on transgressive barriers.

The dominant direction of longshore transport along the Core Banks barrier chain is to the south towards Cape Lookout (Langfelder et al., 1968; Knowles et al., 1973; Fig. 53). Approximately $2.03 \cdot 10^3$ m^3 of sand per year is incorporated into this transport system (Langfelder et al., 1968). This process has aided in dune ridge accretion and elongation of Cape Lookout. The total land area of Cape Lookout has increased from $2.1 \cdot 10^3$ m^2 in 1886 to $4.4 \cdot 10^3$ m^2 in 1955 (Pierce, 1969). However, most of the sand carried by the longshore transport mechanism is apparently deposited on the Cape Lookout shoals, a submarine extension of the subaerially exposed Cape apex (Fig. 53). The shoals extend approximately 28 km offshore and are considered to be a massif marking the retreat path of the cape through Holocene time.

Cape Lookout itself is roughly triangular in shape with active dune ridges up to 10 m in height. A jetty was built off the western shore early in the 1900's, resulting in accretion and formation of a large recurved sand spit, "Power Squadron Spit". This spit has built out into the open water extending northward toward Shackleford Banks (Fig. 53).

Depositional Units and Facies Relationships:

Holocene sediments consist of fine- to coarse-grained sands associated with a prograding cape-shoal

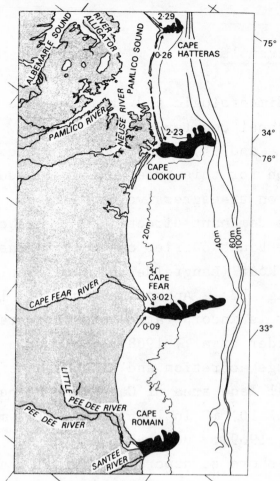

Fig. 52. Cape-associated sand bars, across part of the eastern USA, forming at sites of littoral drift convergence (sand transport rates in yd/yr x 10^{-3}) (in Swift, 1976a).

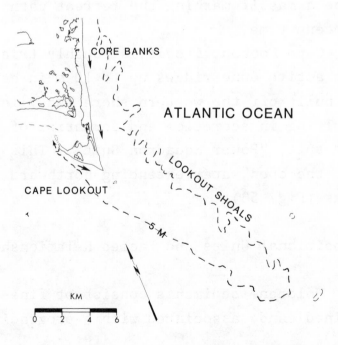

Fig. 53. Diagram of Cape Lookout and the Lookout Shoals along the eastern and southermost portions of the Shackleford and Core Banks barrier limbs. Arrows indicate the dominate direction of longshore transport (from Moslow and Heron, 1981).

complex. These sediments were deposited in recurved
spit, foreshore, shoreface and overwash environments.
A composite vertical sedimentary sequence of the
Cape Lookout shoreface section is shown in Fig. 54. This
is a coarsening upward, burrowed to cross-bedded sequence
that is very similar to the shoreface sequence of
prograding barrier islands.

Locations of drill holes and stratigraphic cross-
sections at Cape Lookout are shown in Fig. 55. Shoreface deposits gradational with beach and dune deposits
extend just offshore from Core Banks and out onto the
Lookout Shoals. These shoreface deposits are similar to
the fine sands and silts found beneath Cape Lookout in the
lower half of the Holocene sequence that are overlain by
storm overwash deposits (Figs. 56 and 57). The vertical
stacking of the shoreface and washover facies depicts a
regressive sequence found only beneath the cape portion
of Core Banks. The shoreface sands beneath Cape Lookout
abut the backbarrier lagoonal sands somewhere between
hole one and four to the north (Fig. 56) marking a major
facies change. The stratigraphic sequence underlying the
Core Banks barrier limb to the northeast is one of
erosional transgression while that sequence beneath
Cape Lookout is one of depositional regression produced
by progradation. This progradation was caused by the
combined effects of washover deposition, a southerly longshore transport and the formation of beach ridges on the
depositional margin of the Cape.

Ancient Example

Shoreline and shelf sandstones of the La Ventana
Tongue (Campanian), in the San Juan Basin of New Mexico
may be an ancient example of a cape-shoal massif. Palmer

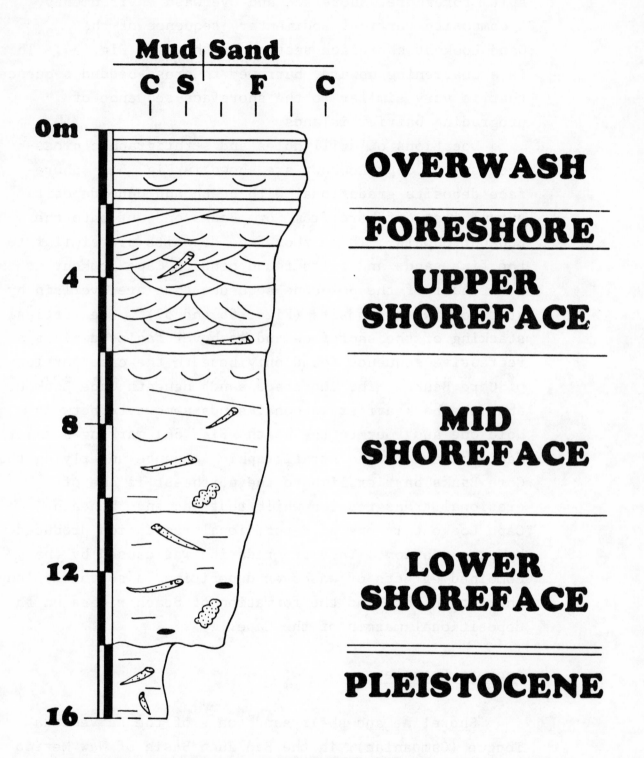

Fig. 54. Composite vertical sedimentary sequence of shoreface deposits at Cape Lookout, North Carolina.

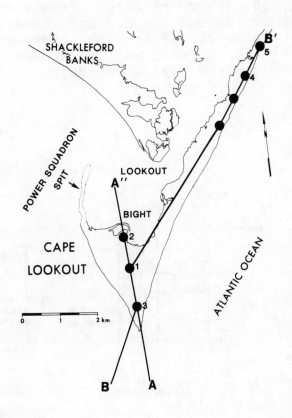

Fig. 55. Location of the drill holes and two lines of
cross-section at Cape Lookout. (from Moslow and Heron, 1981).

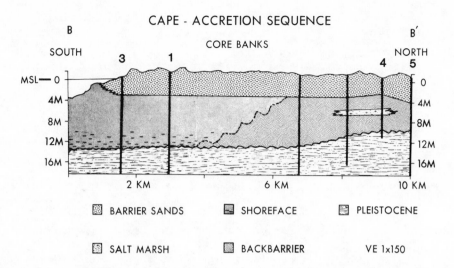

Fig. 56. Shore parallel cross-section B-B' of the Holocene of southern Core Banks and Cape Lookout. An erosive contact marks the facies change from the backbarrier silty sands beneath the Core Banks barrier and the shoreface deposits underlying Cape Lookout (from Moslow and Heron, 1981).

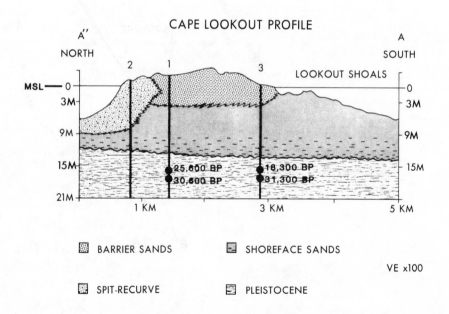

Fig. 57. Cross section A"-A of the late Holocene and upper Pleistocene of the Cape Lookout apex. The section is dominated by a regressive sequence of barrier washover sands overlying shoreface silts and sands. This sequence was produced by the seaward progradation of Cape Lookout (from Moslow and Heron, 1981).

and Scott (1984) have recently described these sandstones as having been deposited in wave-dominated
delta, coastal barrier and shelf sand bar environments,
along the western margin of the Cretaceous Interior
Seaway. The geometries of La Ventana subunits, as
inferred from net sandstone isopachs (Fig. 58), indicate that deposition was associated at least in part
with the reworking of a coastal/deltaic headland and
the formation of a shelf sand bar. The depositional
model for the LaVentana of Palmer and Scott (Fig. 59)
shows many similarities to the Cape Lookout Shoal
complex.

INNER SHELF SHOALS
AND SAND-RIDGES

Recent studies have examined the origin, evolution
and recognitinn of transgressive sand-ridges on the
storm-dominated New Jersey continental shelf
(Stubblefied, et al., 1984; Swift et al., 1984).
While the New Jersey shelf sand-ridges have been intensely
studied, the origin and geologic framework of these
sands is still quite controversial. Prevailing theories
revolve around an origin related to either the drowning
of a barrier island shoreline or the reworking of continental shelf sands. Figueiredo (1984) has summarized
a vast amount of high resolution seismic and some
vibracore data of the New Jersey sand ridges. However,
there is still no consistent depositional model for these
storm-dominated shelf sand-ridges.

A better understanding presently exists for the
origin and geologic framework of sand shoals in a deltaic
setting on the Louisiana continental shelf (Fig. 60). These
shoals are similar in size and shape to some of the sand
ridges on the New Jersey shelf, however, their origin
and internal geometry are quite different. The Louisiana
shelf shoals have recently been examined by Penland et al
(1984) and Suter et al (1984) as part of an ongoing study

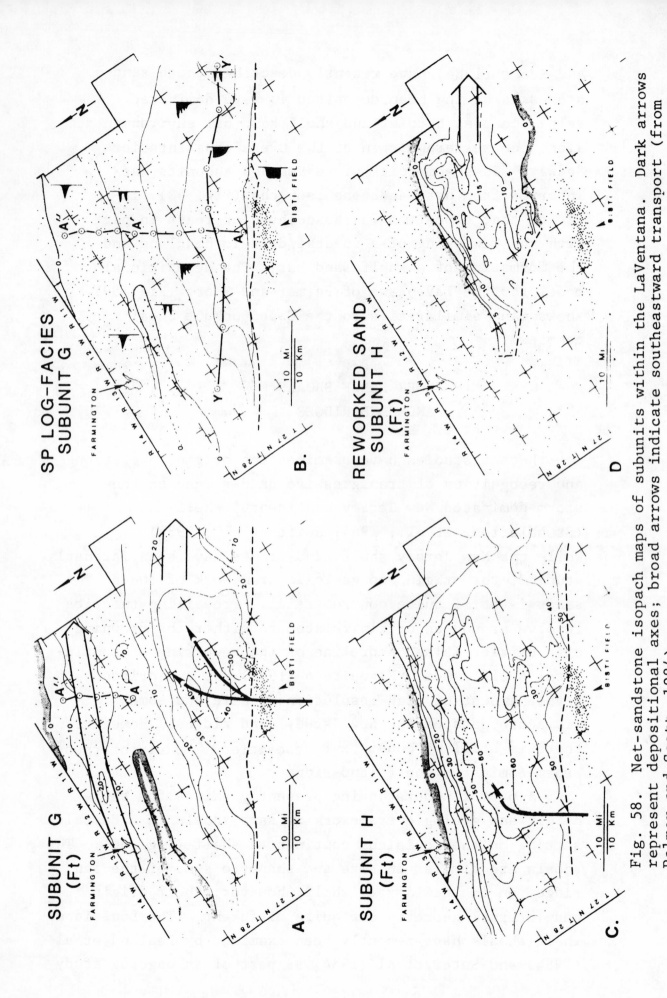

Fig. 58. Net-sandstone isopach maps of subunits within the LaVentana. Dark arrows represent depositional axes; broad arrows indicate southeastward transport (from Palmer and Scott, 1984).

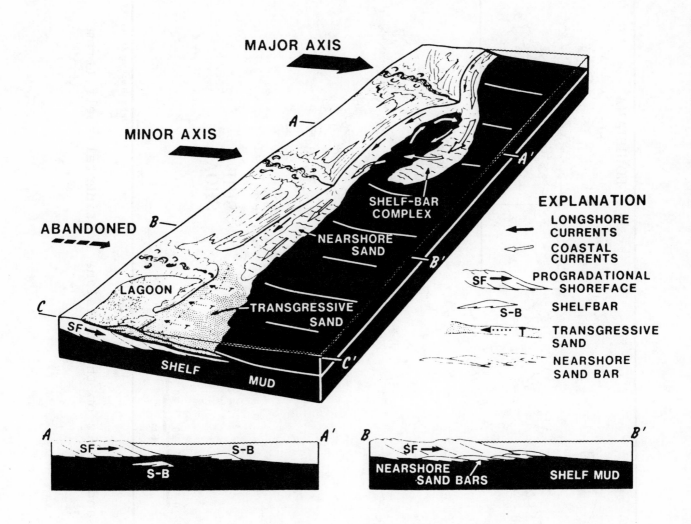

Fig. 59. Model of inferred depositional systems of
La Ventana Tongue (from Palmer and Scott, 1984).

-89-

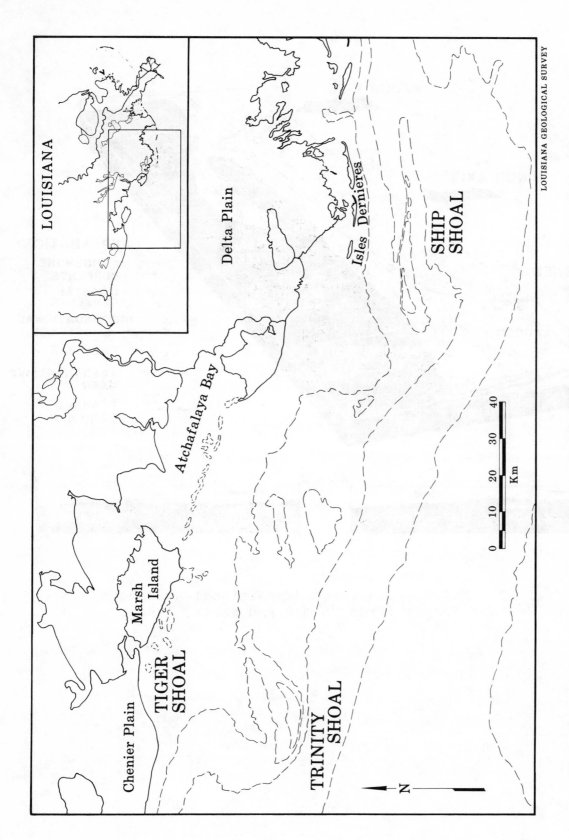

Fig. 60. Location of sand shoals on the Louisiana continental shelf (from Penland et al, 1984).

of shelf geology by the Louisiana Geologic Survey's
Coastal Program.

Modern Example

More than 1000 km of high resolution seismic profiles
correlated with 17 10-12 m vibracores provide the
data base for analyzing the sedimentologic characteristics
of transgressive sand shoals on the Louisiana continental
shelf (Fig. 61). The development of these shoals is
initiated by abandonment of older Holocene complexes
of the Mississippi delta, followed by subsidence-
induced sea level rise. Ship and Trinity Shoals are
the largest of these shelf sand-bodies and provide a
possible modern analogue for some shelf sandstones
of the Cretaceous Western Interior seaway.

Depositional Units and Facies Relationships:

The Ship Shoal sand lies disconformably on the
deltaic muds of the Maringouin complex, abandoned
some 6150 years B.P. The shoal is asymmetric landward,
32 km long , and 2-4 km wide. Relief ranges from
2-6 m from east to west, with a corresponding decrease
in water depth over the shoal crest from -6 to -3 m.
Maximum sand body thickness is 7 m in the western region,
pinching out seaward on the erosional inner shelf and
terminated landward by a depositional surface. Internally,
the shoal is characterized by very low angle landward-
dipping clinoform reflectors, while the underlying
deltaic sequence contains low angle seaward dipping
clinoforms. Numerous small channels occur below the
shoal in the western area, although no large channels
were seen on seismic profiles. Cores show a 3-7 m thick

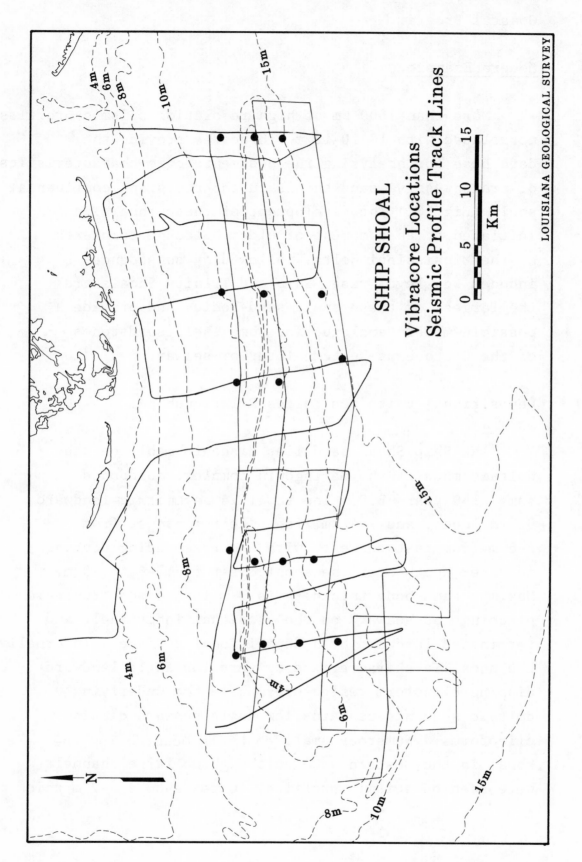

Fig. 61. Location of seismic track lines and vibracore holes on Ship Shoal (from Suter et al, 1984).

coarsening upward sequence of fine grained sand and
shell, overlying a dark, organic rich, silty clay;
burrowing is very rare in the muddy units (Fig. 62).

The shoal sand package is comprised of three
depositional units (Fig. 62):1). The back shoal:
an interbedded sequence of laminated to burrowed
silty-sands and wavy bedded to burrowed silty
clays (Fig. 63); 2) The lower shoal: a coarsening
upward sequence of massive appearing, burrowed and
laminated sands; and 3) the shoal crest: a fine
medium grained sequence with horizontal laminations,
graded storm layers, lithoclasts and rare Ophiomorpha
burrows (Fig. 63).

Trinity Shoal is associated with the Teche complex,
abandoned some 3500 years B.P. The shoal is a lunate,
shore parallel feature some 36 km long and 5-10 km wide.
Relief ranges east-west from 2-3 m, with a corresponding
decrease east-west in water depth over the shoal crest
from -5 to -2 m. The Trinity Shoal sand body is 5-7 m
thick, and is composed internally of a set of low angle
westward dipping clinoform reflectors. Three levels of
channeling related to sea level changes in the Early
Wisconsinan, Late Wisconsinan, and Holocene (Maringouin
delta) underlie and occur seaward of Trinity Shoal.
Continued sedimentation of the modern Atchafalaya Delta
will soon encase Trinity Shoal in mud.

Ancient Example

The Cretaceous Shannon Sandstone in the Hartzog
Draw Field, Powder River Basin, Wyoming (Fig. 64)
has been interpreted as a continental shelf sand
(Tillman and Martinsen, 1984). The Hartzog Draw
sandstone reservoir was deposited as one, or a series

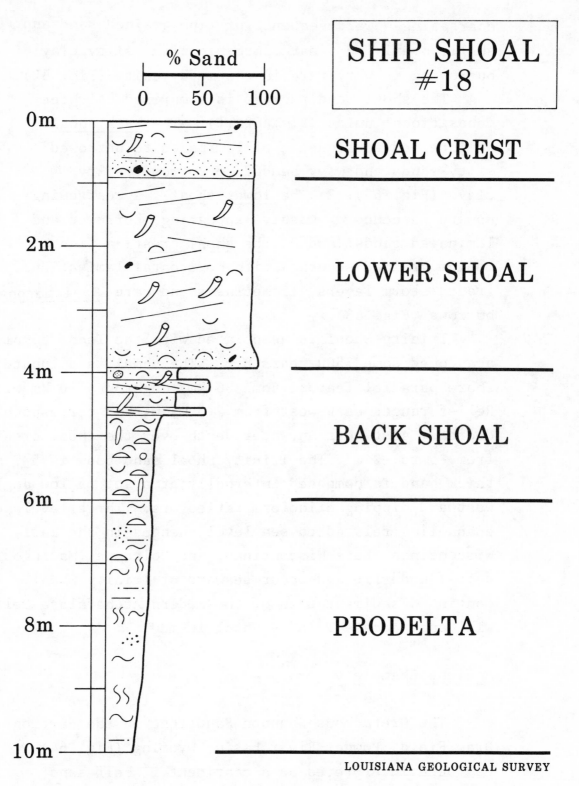

% Sand

0   50   100

SHIP SHOAL
#18

SHOAL CREST

LOWER SHOAL

BACK SHOAL

PRODELTA

LOUISIANA GEOLOGICAL SURVEY

Fig. 62. Vertical sedimentary sequence of cored deposits through Ship Shoal (from Penland et al, 1984)

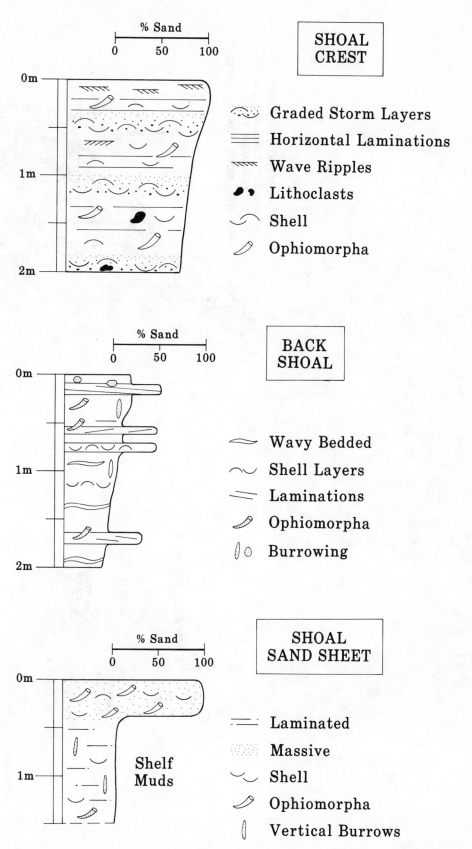

Fig. 63. Schematic core descriptions of three sedimentary facies in the Ship Shoal shelf sand body (from Suter et al, 1984).

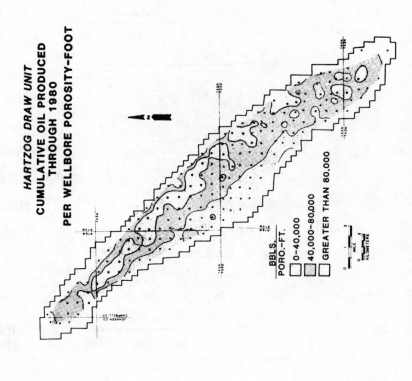

Fig. 65. Primary oil production contour map (from Hearn et al., 1984).

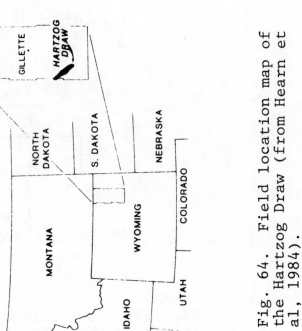

Fig. 64. Field location map of the Hartzog Draw (from Hearn et al, 1984).

of, shelf sand ridges in water depths of 60-300 ft.
in the Western Interior seaway. It is estimated
to have 350 million bbls of oil in place and is
completely encased in the Cody Shale with a structural
dip of 1° to 2°, thereby forming a pure stratigraphic
trap (Hearn et al., 1984) (Fig. 65).

Reservoir geometry and sedimentary facies of the
Shannon Sandstone in the central part of the Hartzog
Draw Field was examined in detail by Tye et al (1983).
This study is summarized in Hearn et al (1984), and
divides the Shannon Sandstone into a number of litho-
logic units. Strike and dip stratigraphic cross-
sections (Fig. 66) show the internal geometry and
facies relationships for this Cretaceous shelf sandstone. The "Middle Lens" shandstone in the cross-
section (Fig. 66) is interpreted as the Central Bar
Facies of the shelf sand ridge. This is the facies of
highest reservoir quality and is a cross-bedded
medium-fine grained sandstone with scattered clasts
of mudstone and minor shale laminae (Tillman and
Martinsen, 1984; Hearn et al., 1984). The central
bar facies is probably analogous to the combined
lower shoal and shoal crest facies of the modern
Louisiana continental shelf (Figs. 67 and 62).

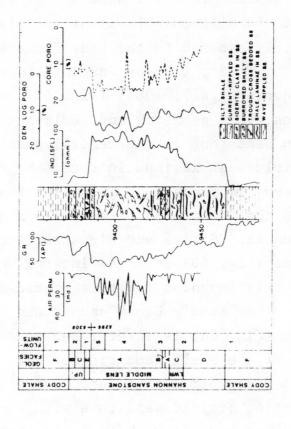

Fig. 67. Composite reservoir quality profile of the "Middle Lens" (Central Bar Facies) in the Hartzog Draw (from Hearn et al., 1984).

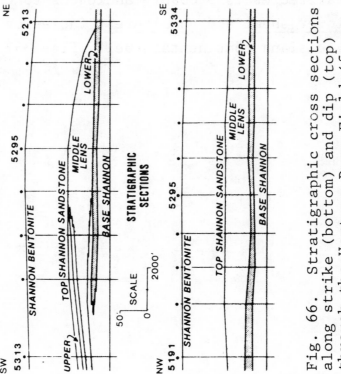

Fig. 66. Stratigraphic cross sections along strike (bottom) and dip (top) through the Hartzog Draw Field (from Hearn et al., 1984).

REFERENCES

Barwis, J. H. and Hayes, M. O., 1979, Regional patterns of modern barrier island and tidal inlet deposition as applies to paleoenvironmental studies: In: J. C. Ferm and J. C. Horne (Editors), Carboniferous Depositional Environments of the Appalachian Region. Spec. Pub., Univ. South Carolina Coal Group, p. 472-498.

Berelson, W. M., 1979, Barrier island evolution and its effect on lagoonal sedimentation: Shackleford Banks, Back Sound and Harkers Island: Cape Lookout National Seashore. Thesis, Duke University, Durham, N. C., 132p. (unpublished).

Berg, R. R., and Davies, D. K., 1968, Origin of Lower Cretaceous Muddy Sandstone at Belle Creek Field, Montana: American Association Petroleum Geologists Bulletin, v. 52, no. 20, p. 1888-1898.

Davies, D. K., Ethridge, F. G., and Berg, R. R., 1971, Recognition of barrier environments: American Association Petroleum Geologist Bulletin, p. 550-565.

Figueiredo, A. G., 1984, Submarine sand ridges: geology and development, New Jersey, U.S.A.: Dissertation, University of Miami, Coral Gables, Florida, 408p. (unpublished).

Fischer, A. G., 1961, Stratigraphic record of transgressing seas in light of sedimentation on Atlantic coast of New Jersey: Amer. Assoc. Petrol. Geol. Bull., v. 45, p. 1656-1666.

Hayes, M. O., 1975, Morphology of sand accumulation in estuaries: an introduction to the symposium: in Estuarine Research, II: Geology and Engineering (Ed. by L. E. Cronin), p. 3-22. Academic Press, London.

Hayes, M. O. and Kana, T. W., 1976, Terrigenous Clastic Depositional Environments - Some Modern Examples, p. 1-131, Tech. Rept. 11-CRD, Coastal Res. Div., University South Carolina.

Hearn, C. L., Ebanks, W. J. Jr., Tye, R. S. and Ranganathan, V., 1984, Geological factors influencing reservoir performance of the Hartzog Draw Field, Wyoming: Journal of Petroleum Technology, p. 1335-1344.

Herbert, J. R., 1979. Post-Miocene stratigraphy and evolution of northern Core Banks, North Carolina. Thesis, Duke University, 166 p. (unpublished).

Heron, S. D., Jr., Moslow, T. F., Berelson, W. M., Herbert, J. R., Steele, G. A., and Susman, K. R., 1984, Holocene sedimentation of a wave-dominated barrier island shoreline: Cape Lookout, North Carolina: Marine Geology.

Horne, J. C. and Ferm, J. C., 1976, Carboniferous Depositional environments in the Pocohontas Basin, eastern Kentucky and southern West Virginia: Amer. Assoc. Petrol. Geol. Field Trip Guidebook, Dept. Geol., University South Carolina, 129p.

Houbolt, J.J.H.C., 1968, Recent sediments in the southern bight of the North Sea: Geol.. Mijnb, 47: 245-273.

Johnson, H. D., 1978, Shallow siliclastic seas: in H. B. Reading (ed.), Sedimentary Environments and Facies, Elsevier, New York, 207-258.

Jordan, D. W., Helmold, K. P. and Moslow, T. F., 1981, Storm washover deposition on the Texas Gulf Coast by Hurricane Allen, 1980 and application to stratigraphic traps: Cities Service Research Report No. 94, G81-20, 61p.

Knowles, C. E., Langfelder, J. and McDonald, R., 1973, A preliminary study of storm included beach erosion for North Carolina: Rep. 73-75, Center for Marine Coastal Studies, North Carolina State University, Raleigh, North Carolina.

Land, C. B., Jr., 1972, Stratigraphy of Fox Hills Sandstone and associated Formations, Rock Springs Uplift and Wamsutter Arch area, Sweetwater County, Wyoming: a shoreline-estuary sandstone model for the Late Cretaceous: Colorado School of Mines Quarterly, v. 67, no. 2, 69p.

Langfelder, J., Stafford, D. and Amein, M., 1968, A reconnaissance of coastal erosion in North Carolina: Dept. Civil Eng., North Carolina State University, Raleigh, North Carolina, 127p.

McCubbin, D. G., 1982, Barrier island and strand-plain facies: in P.A. Scholle and D. Spearing (eds.), Sandstone Depositional Environments: Amer. Assoc. Petr. Geols., Memoir No. 31, p. 247-279.

McGregor, A. A., and Biggs, C. A., 1968, Bell Creek Field, Montana: a rich stratigraphic trap: American Association Petroleum Geologist Bulletin, v. 52, no. 10, 1869-1887.

Moslow, T. F., 1980, Mesotidal barrier island stratigraphy: unpub. Ph.D. Diss., University South Carolina, Columbia, South Carolina, 247p.

Moslow, T. F. and Colquhoun, D. J., 1981, Influence of sea level change on barrier island evolution: Oceanis, 7: 439-454.

Moslow, T. F. and Heron, S. D., 1978. Relict inlets: preservation and occurrence in the Holocene stratigraphy of southern Core Banks, North Carolina: Jour. Sed. Petrol., 48: no. 4, 1275-1286.

Moslow, T. F., and Heron, S. D., 1979, Quaternary evolution of
Core Banks, North Carolina: Cape Lookout to New Drum Inlet:
in, Leatherman, S. P., ed., Barrier Islands: from the Gulf of
St. Lawrence to the Gulf of Mexico, Academic Press, p. 211-236.

Moslow, T. F. and Heron, S. D., 1981, Holocene depositional history
of a microtidal cuspate foreland cape: Cape Lookout, North
Carolina: Marine Geology, v. 41, p. 251-270.

Moslow, T. F. and Tye, R. S., 1984, Sedimentology and stratigraphy
of tidal inlet deposits: Marine Geology.

Palmer, J. J., and Scott, A. J. 1984, Stacked shoreline and shelf
sandstone of the LaVentana Tounge (Campanian), Northwestern
New Mexico: Amer. Assoc, Petr. Geol., v. 68, no. 1, p. 74-91.

Penland, S. and Boyd, R., 1981, Shoreline changes on the Louisiana
barrier coast: IEEE Oceans, Marine Technology Society and IEEE
(Ocenaography Section), 209-219.

Penland, S. and Boyd, R., in press, Transgressive Depositional
Environments of the Mississippi River Delta: A Guide to the
Barrier Islands, Beaches and Shoals in Louisiana: Geol. Soc.
America, 1982 National Meeting, Field Trip Guidebook No. 7.

Penland, S., Nummedal, D., and Roberts, H., 1981, Deltaic barrier
development on the Louisiana coast: Gulf Coast Assoc. Trans.,
471-476.

Penland, S. P., Suter, J. R., and Moslow, T. F., 1984, Sand shoal
development on the muddy Mississippi Delta shelf: Amer. Assoc.
Petr. Geol. Bull., abs., v. 68, no. 4, p. 515.

Pierce, J. W., 1969, Sediment budget along a barrier island chain:
Sediment. Geol. 3: 5-16.

Price, W. A. and Parker, R. H., 1979, Origins of permanent inlets
separating barrier islands and influence of drowned valleys on
tidal records along the Gulf Coast of Texas: Trans. G.C.A.G.S.:
v. 29, 371-385.

Reinson, G. E., 1979, Barrier island systems: in, R. G. Walker (ed.),
Facies Models, Geol. Assoc. Canada, Reprint Series 1, 57-74.

Stubblefield, W. L., McGrail, D. W., and Kersey, D. G., 1984,
Recognition of transgressive and post-transgressive sand ridges
on the New Jersey continental shelf: in, R. W. Tillman and C. T.
Siemers, Siliciclastic Shelf Sediments: Soc. Econ. Paleon.
and Miner., Special Publ. No. 34, p. 1-24.

Suter, J. R., Penland, S., and Moslow, T. F., 1984, Geologic framework of sand shoals on the muddy Mississippi Delta shelf: abs., Amer. Assoc. Petr. Geol. Bull., v. 68, no. 4, p. 533.

Swift, D.J.P., Duane, D. B. and McKinney, T. F., 1973, Ridge and swale topography of the Middle Atlantic Bight, North America: secular response to the Holocene hydraulic regime: Mar. Geol., 15: 227-247.

Swift, D.J.P., 1976, Coastal sedimentation: in D. J. Stanley and D.J.P. Swift (eds.), Marine Sediment Transport and Environmental Management, John Wiley and Sons, New York, 225-310.

Swift, D.J.P., McKinney, T. F., and Stahl, L., 1984, Recognition of transgressive and post-transgressive sand ridges on the New Jersey continental shelf: in, R. W. Tillman and C. T. Siemers, Siliciclastic shelf Sediments: SEPM Special Pub., no. 34, p. 25-36.

Tillman, R. W. and Martinsen, R. S., 1984, The Shannon shelf-ridge sandstone complex, Salt Creek Anticline area, Powder River Basin, Wyoming: in R. W. Tillman and C. T. Siemers, eds., Siliciclastic Shelf Sediments: SEPM Special Pub., no. 34, p. 85-142.

Tye, R. S., 1981, Geomorphic evolution and stratigraphic framework of Price and Capers Inlets, South Carolina: unpub. M.S. thesis, University South Carolina, 144p.

Tye, R. S., 1984, Geomorphic evolution and stratigraphy of Price and Capers Inlets, South Carolina: Sedimentology.

Tye, R. S., Ranganathan, V., and Ebanks, W. J., Jr., 1983, Stratigraphic reservoir analysis of the Shannon Sandstone, Hartzog Draw Field, Campbell and Johnson Counties, Wyoming: Cities Service Research Report No. RMG83-03, 147p.

Tye, R. S. and Moslow, T. F., submitted, Sand-body geometry and stratigraphy of tidal inlet deposits: Amer. Assoc. Pet. Geol. Bull.

Van Horn, M. D., 1979 Stratigraphy of the Almond Formation, east-central flank of the Rock Springs Uplift, Sweetwater County, Wyoming: A Mesotidal-Shoreline Model for the Late Cretaceous: unpub. M.S. thesis (T 1955), Colo. School of Mines, 150p.

Weimer, R. J. and Tillman, R. W., 1980, Tectonic Influence on deltaic shoreline facies, Fox Hills Sandstone, West-Central Denver Basin: Colorado School of Mines, Professional Contribution No. 10, 131p.

Weimer, R. J. and Tillman, R. W., 1982, Sandstone reservoirs: Journal of Petroleum Technology, 13p.